THE RACIAL POLICIES OF AMERICAN INDUSTRY

REPORT NO. 12

THE NEGRO
IN THE MEAT INDUSTRY

by

WALTER A. FOGEL

Associate Professor of Industrial Relations
University of California, Los Angeles

Published by
INDUSTRIAL RESEARCH UNIT, DEPARTMENT OF INDUSTRY
Wharton School of Finance and Commerce
University of Pennsylvania

Distributed by
University of Pennsylvania Press
Philadelphia, Pennsylvania 19104

Copyright © 1970 by the Trustees of the University of Pennsylvania
Library of Congress Catalog Card Number 71-116622
SBN: 8122-9049-6
MANUFACTURED IN THE UNITED STATES OF AMERICA

FOREWORD

In September 1966, the Ford Foundation announced a major grant to the Industrial Research Unit of the Wharton School to fund studies of the Racial Policies of American Industry. The purpose of the research effort, now in its third year, is to determine why some industries are more hospitable to the employment of Negroes than are others and why some companies within the same industry have vastly different racial employment policies, and to propose appropriate policy.

The studies have proceeded on an industry-by-industry basis, under the direction of the undersigned, with Dr. Richard L. Rowan, Associate Professor of Industry, as Associate Director. In addition, both Dr. Rowan and the undersigned have undertaken specific industry studies. This study of the meat industry is the twelfth in a series of reports dealing with specific industries; others already published include the automobile, aerospace, steel, hotel, petroleum, rubber tire, chemical, and paper industries. Studies of the banking, insurance, and public utility industries are either in press or in the pre-press editing stage. Studies of the textile, tobacco, department store, motor, rail, and air transport industries, among others, are scheduled for completion shortly. We are also publishing several volumes combining and comparing the findings of the various studies. This report will be contained in the third manufacturing industry volume.

The author of this study, Dr. Walter A. Fogel, has already exhibited his keen insight and careful interest in minority problems and industrial race relations by research into the problems of Mexican-Americans. A native of the Midwest, he received his doctorate in economics at Massachusetts Institute of Technology before joining the faculty of the University of California, Los Angeles, where he is now Associate Professor of Industrial Relations.

Labor relations in the meat industry have been the subject of an unusual amount of published material. The author wishes to acknowledge especially his debt to two: Alma Herbst's, *The*

Negro in the Slaughtering and Meat Packing Industry in Chicago, written in the 1920's; and Theodore Purcell's, *Blue Collar Man,* published in 1960. These books represent the two kinds of historical material which the author was also able to bring together—general history pertaining to Negroes in the meat industry and information about the conditions of Negro employment within meat plants. The author supplemented the published material with interviews and statistics obtained in a field survey. He wishes to record his debt to the many company and union officials, employees of meat establishments, and persons associated with community organizations for their discussions of various aspects of Negro employment.

The manuscript was checked and edited and the index made by Mrs. Marie R. Keeney. Robert C. Gulledge and John C. Howard developed and checked most of the statistical data. Mrs. Margaret E. Doyle, Administrative Assistant of the Industrial Research Unit, cared for the numerous administrative details associated with this and all of the Unit's other activities. Errors or shortcomings are, of course, the sole responsibility of the author.

In most previous reports, as in this one, the data cited as "in the possession of the author," have been carefully authenticated and are on file in our Industrial Research Unit library.

HERBERT R. NORTHRUP, *Director*
Industrial Research Unit
Wharton School of Finance and Commerce
University of Pennsylvania

Philadelphia
January 1970

TABLE OF CONTENTS

LIST OF TABLES

APPENDIX TABLES

CHAPTER I.

Introduction

This volume is an attempt to tell the full story of Negro employment in the meat industry, from the time that black workers first came into the industry up to the present. Its focus, then, is the history and the contemporary status of Negroes in the meat industry. It is concerned, in both historical and contemporary senses, with numbers of Negroes employed; their occupational and related statuses; and industry, union, and government practices which have influenced these matters.

The inclusion of considerable historical material as well as current analysis in this, as in other studies in this series, reflects our belief that the rapidly increasing output of studies of minority employment problems will be enhanced in value if they give adequate attention to history. The history should be not only that of the industry or other employing unit, but also that of the socioeconomic environments in which the industry has operated so that connections can be made between these environments and minority employment status. Another function served by telling the history of Negro employment in an industry is to put what is happening now into the perspective of what has gone on before. Current developments are better understood and judged if one is familiar with the relevant past.

The meat industry is of special interest in the study of the Racial Policies of American Industry for a number of reasons. It was one of the very first of the big-city industries to utilize Negro labor on a large scale. Moreover, the jobs became over time relatively well paid although distinctly unpleasant in many aspects. In this industry, also, Negroes have played key roles in labor relations, both as strikebreakers and as union members. And in meat packing, perhaps more than in any other industry, the racial policies of the industry importantly affected race relations in the communities where the plants were located. Finally, recent years have seen the virtual disappearance of the large, big-city slaughtering establishments and the substitution therefor of smaller establishments near the source of meat supply areas, where, unlike in the cities, few Negroes dwell. Meanwhile, there has developed in the South a burgeoning chicken industry employing largely Negro female labor.

The story of the Negro's role and status in this significant and evolving industry is recounted in the bulk of this study. Before such discussion, however, it is important to understand the basic industry background.

CHAPTER II

The Meat Industry

"Meat Products" is the term given to the meat manufacturing industry by governmental Standard Industrial Classification (SIC) system and by the United States Bureau of the Census. The divisions of the industry together with their definitions and SIC code numbers are set forth in Table 1.

TABLE 1. *Meat Industry, Standard Industrial Classification Definitions*

---

201 Meat Products

2011 *Meat packing plants.* Establishments primarily engaged in the slaughtering of meat (cattle, hogs, lambs, calves, and other animals, except small game) which is to be sold or processed on the same premises.

2013 *Sausages and other prepared meats* (meat processing). Establishments primarily engaged in manufacturing sausages, cured meats, smoked meats, canned meats, frozen meats, other prepared meats, and meat specialties, from purchased carcasses and other materials.

2015 *Poultry and small game dressing and packing, wholesale.* Establishments primarily engaged in killing, dressing, packing and canning poultry, rabbits and other small game.

Source: U.S. Bureau of the Budget, *Standard Industrial Classification Manual* (Washington: Government Printing Office, 1967), pp. 42-43.

Historically, the meat industry outside the activities of raising and marketing livestock has been associated with meat packing —the slaughtering of animals in abattoirs and the preparation of various kinds of meat products in adjacent facilities. People employed in these activities worked for "packinghouses." Poultry establishments and meat processing plants not adjacent to abattoirs were uncommon until the 1920's. By the end of the Great Depression, however, meat and poultry processing had become sufficiently important to justify their recognition by government agencies as distinct sectors of the meat industry, along with the much older meat packing division.

Meat packing is still the largest division of the meat industry, although poultry processing has grown very rapidly in the last twenty years. In 1947, meat packing employed three-quarters of all meat industry workers, compared to 8 percent in poultry and 16 percent in meat processing. By 1967, the meat packing share of employment had declined to 57 percent, while poultry processing employed 27 percent of all workers and the meat processing share had remained constant.[1] These changes in the composition of the meat industry reflect improved technologies of meat and poultry processing, and concomitant changes in consumption patterns.

The development of poultry processing means that the meat industry now includes divisions which have little in common other than the fact that they all produce meat products of one kind or another. On the dimensions of size of establishment, location, wages, and unionization, as well as others, the meat packing and poultry divisions are far apart, with meat processing quite close to the former in terms of wages but similar to the latter with respect to plant size. Unfortunately, Negro employment data are not available separately for each of the divisions, although in Chapters V and VII inferences are made concerning Negro employment in the poultry and meat packing divisions from other information which is available.

INDUSTRIAL STRUCTURE

Table 2 lists employment, payrolls, and other pertinent statistics for the meat industry and its principal subdivisions. Meat packing remains the largest sector of the industry in terms of number of employees and payrolls as well as in value of shipments. We shall note below, however, that employment in this sector has declined substantially during the last decade. Moreover, the heavy investment in plant and equipment has proved a burden to the older meat firms particularly. Return on such investments has declined in recent years. In 1966, for example, earnings for the industry as a ratio of net worth were only 6.5 percent compared with 13.1 percent for all manufacturing.[2] This poor profitability has encouraged meat firms to close large

---

[1] See Table 5, p. 11.

[2] American Meat Institute, *Financial Facts about the Meat Packing Industry* (Chicago: The Institute, 1967), p. 34.

facilities in cities such as Chicago, Omaha, Kansas City, and St. Louis, in favor of small, highly automated plants near the source of supply.[3] The net effect has been a movement of the packers away from concentrations of Negro population.

TABLE 2. *Meat Industry, Employment, Payrolls, Capital Expenditures, and Other Data, by Standard Industrial Classification*
1967

	Meat Products (SIC 201)	Meat Packing (SIC 2011)	Meat Processing (SIC 2013)	Poultry (SIC 2015)
Total Employees	305,000	174,000	50,000	81,000
	Millions of Dollars			
Payrolls	1,910	1,265	350	295
Value added by manufacture	3,414	2,191	683	540
Cost of materials	17,370	13,177	1,945	2,248
Value of shipments	20,776	15,355	2,633	2,788
Capital expenditures, new	195	129	28	38

Source: *U.S. Census of Manufactures 1967*, Series MC 67(P)-1, Summary Series, Preliminary Report, April 1969.

Data for the twelve largest meat firms are set forth in Table 3 for 1968, or earlier if the more recent data are not available. The poor profit records of most of the older companies are clear. It is unlikely that the listings of the twelve largest companies in any other industry for this prosperous year would have found three of them, including the biggest, operating at a loss, and the second largest netting profits of only 4.1 percent of invested capital.

These twelve largest firms employ one-third to 40 percent of the industry's total personnel. The share of meat industry employment and sales held by the largest firms has been declining steadily since World War II, as an increasing number of small

---

[3] See Harold B. Meyers, "For the Old Meatpackers, Things are Tough All Over," *Fortune*, Vol. LXXIX (February 1969), pp. 89-93, 134, 136.

TABLE 3. *The Twelve Largest Meat Companies*
1968 Statistics

Company and 1968 Rank among Industrial Corporations	Headquarters	Sales	Assets	Net Income	Invested Capital	Number of Employees	Net Income as a Percent of	
		(000)					Sales	Invested Capital
Swift (24)	Chicago	$2,827,127	$734,888	$(41,567)[a]	$357,417	46,200	—	—
Armour [b] (38)	Chicago	2,096,402	560,469	12,029	291,777	32,800	0.6	4.1
Wilson [c] (81)	Chicago	990,860	196,210	12,905	121,983	18,000	1.3	10.6
Morrell [d] (99)	Chicago	811,551	102,065	1,911	53,397	12,264	0.2	3.6
Hormel (166)	Austin, Minn.	585,879	108,484	9,134	70,220	8,292	1.6	13.0
Iowa Beef Packers (185)	Dakota City, Neb.	533,861	69,253	5,453	29,308	2,200	1.0	18.6
Oscar Mayer (202)	Madison, Wis.	481,880	115,449	11,775	89,830	10,577	2.4	13.1
Hygrade Food Products (249)	Detroit	370,630	61,319	(4,072)[a]	10,950	5,400	—	—
Cudahy (273)	Phoenix	333,729	66,758	6,856	38,601	5,600	2.1	17.8
Rath Packing (347)	Waterloo, Iowa	236,032	37,346	(694)[a]	9,446	4,830	—	—
Needham Packing (417)	Sioux City, Iowa	180,195	11,947	1,212	7,635	661	0.7	15.9
American Beef Packers (491)	Oakland, Iowa	147,205	15,307	930	3,952	700	0.6	23.5

Source: *Fortune*, Vol. LXXIX (May 15, 1969), pp. 168-185; and Vol. LXXV (June 15, 1967), pp. 198-201.

[a] Loss.

[b] Taken over by General Host and Greyhound Corporation, 1969.

[c] 1966 data and rank. Taken over by Ling-Temco-Vought, 1967.

[d] 1966 data and rank. Taken over by AMK Corporation, 1967.

firms oriented to local and regional markets have developed.[4] Some of the data in Table 3 pertains to non-meat business activities of the larger companies resulting from expansion into other areas of interest, but at least 85 percent of the total sales of these companies came from meat in 1968.[5] As Table 3 also indicates, the older meat concerns, with their low earnings and high ratios of fixed assets, are prime targets for takeovers by conglomerates. Three have already been gobbled up and Swift and Rath have had passes made to merge them. Mergers are accelerated by tax advantages for the surviving corporation, but are also prompted by the belief that more innovative management could improve profitability.[6] Certainly the record of new firms, such as Iowa Beef Packers or American Beef Packers, seems to indicate that profits can be made in the industry.

Both the threat of takeovers and the rise of new firms have quickened the readjustment of the industry to new plants outside of the large cities. New managements, or old managements running scared, are hastening to close the outmoded plants and put up new ones in the rural Midwest; this is where the new concerns are found. And this is not where Negroes largely dwell.

Today the large, multipurpose plant employing 5,000 to 15,-000 is extinct. More than 50 percent of all meat packing plant workers are employed in establishments of 500 employees or more, but the largest of these plants employ only 3,000 to 4,000 persons. The trend is toward the specialized, highly mechanized facilities employing relatively few workers.[7]

Processed meat and poultry plants are typically small operations employing less than 250 employees. Poultry operations are especially significant in the South where black women are a major segment of their employee force.

Industrial Location

We have already noted that the industry has been moving away from the large midwestern cities for several years. These

---

[4] National Commission on Food Marketing, *Organization and Competition in the Livestock and Meat Industry* (Washington: U.S. Government Printing Office, 1966), Chapters 2-6.

[5] Based on company annual reports.

[6] Meyers, *loc. cit.* We shall raise the question below whether more innovative management could improve Negro job opportunities.

[7] Data from U.S. Census of Manufacturers. See also Meyers, *loc. cit.*

cities became the center of the industry because, in the late
nineteenth and early twentieth centuries, most livestock and livestock products were shipped by rail. Therefore, the meat industry developed in midwestern cities which were terminals for
railroads that ran through cattle-raising areas. Chicago, St.
Louis, Greater Kansas City, Omaha, and a few smaller cities
became the centers of the industry. With the development of
improved highways and truck transportation, beginning in the
1920's, meat packing activity began a movement away from the
large cities to the less populated areas where livestock are
raised. Iowa and Minnesota have been the states which gained
most from this decentralization; these two states and contiguous
areas now contain most of the country's large meat packing
plants. There has also been movement of the meat industry
to the South and the West. The major gains for the southern
meat industry have come from the poultry division—almost 60
percent of all poultry employment is now located in the South.
(Table 4.)

These shifts in industry location have obvious implications for
Negro employment. Most Negroes in the North live in large
metropolitan areas, so any movement of plants to smaller cities
reduces their job opportunities. Moreover, the sector of the
country to which the meat packing industry has migrated has
one of the lowest percentages of Negro population in the United
States. On the other hand, the development of the southern part
of the industry has added to Negro job opportunities, although
most of the gains have come in the low-wage poultry division.
Table 4 gives the distribution of meat industry employment for
the regions which will be referred to in this report, and also
shows the states included in each region.

The odors and unpleasant characteristics of meat plants have
encouraged their location away from the centers of cities in
recent years. Negro settlements grew up around many of the
old meat packing establishments, but newer plants, like those
in other industries, now are often located away from the centers
of population.

TABLE 4. Meat Industry
Employment by Region and Industry Group
1963

Region	Meat Products (SIC 201)		Meat Packing (SIC 2011)		Meat Processing (SIC 2013)		Poultry (SIC 2015)	
	Number	Percent of U.S.	Number	Percent of U.S.	Number	Percent of U.S.	Number	Percent of U.S.
Northeast	39,130	13.1	15,795	8.7	16,823	34.6	6,512	9.3
East North Central	56,474	18.9	36,104	20.0	14,913	30.7	5,457	7.8
West North Central	82,138	27.4	67,929	37.6	3,259	6.7	10,950	15.6
South	89,862	30.0	41,534	23.0	7,225	14.9	41,103	58.6
West	31,972	10.7	19,511	10.8	6,379	13.1	6,082	8.7
Total U. S.	299,576	100.0	180,873	100.0	48,599	100.0	70,104	100.0

Source: *U.S. Census of Manufacturers, 1963,* Vol. II, *Industry Statistics,* Part 1, Meat Products, Table 2.

Definitions of Regions:

Northeast: Connecticut, Maine, Massachusetts, New Hampshire, Rhode Island, Vermont, New York, New Jersey, Pennsylvania.

East North Central: Illinois, Indiana, Michigan, Ohio, Wisconsin.

West North Central: Iowa, Kansas, Minnesota, Missouri, Nebraska, North Dakota, South Dakota.

South: Alabama, Arkansas, Delaware, District of Columbia, Georgia, Florida, Kentucky, Louisiana, Maryland, Mississippi, North Carolina, Oklahoma, South Carolina, Tennessee, Texas, Virginia, West Virginia.

West: Alaska, Arizona, California, Colorado, Hawaii, Idaho, Montana, Nevada, New Mexico, Oregon, Utah, Washington, Wyoming.

MANPOWER

Total employment in the meat industry has been relatively stable during recent years, varying from 315,000 to 330,000. But this over-all figure obscures the rather drastic changes that have occurred within sectors and regions. As Table 5 shows, production employment in meat packing declined from 167,200 in 1951 to 133,000 in 1967 and that in meat processing declined from 38,000 to 37,000, whereas employment in poultry increased from 28,900 to 74,000 in the same period. These employment changes, as already noted, have accompanied the transfer of the meat packing sector from the urban to the rural Midwest and the rise of the poultry sector in the South. Moreover, they occurred despite a steady increase in the per capita consumption of red meat products, especially beef, from approximately 144 pounds in 1958 to an estimated 181 pounds in 1969.[8] The productivity increases which permit the meat packing sector of the industry to produce more with less personnel are likely to be continued. The recently enacted Wholesome Meat Act is adding to the economic incentives in the industry to build and to install the most modern plants and equipment, which are usually easy to maintain according to sanitary standards. Thus, according to a recent government report:

> To meet the changing demands of the consumer, the industry will have to make great strides in plant modernization and utilization. Many new plants are being built near the source of animal supply; the older, larger packer terminals are on the decline.
> New plants are being automated for greater efficiency. They encompass the entire meat preparation industry. . . . These new processes are increasing employee output and showing a beneficial effect on profit margins.[9]

---

[8] U.S. Department of Commerce, Business and Defense Services Administration, *U.S. Industrial Outlook 1969* (Washington: Government Printing Office, 1968), p. 64.

[9] *Ibid.*, pp. 65-66.

TABLE 5. *Meat Industry*
Employment by Standard Industrial Classification, 1939-1967
(000)

	All Employees	Production Workers			
	Total Meat Products	Total Meat Products	Meat Packing	Meat Processing	Poultry
1939	n.a.	146.6	115.0	17.6	14.0
1947	274.4	220.7	167.1	34.5	19.1
1948	n.a.	n.a.	n.a.	n.a.	n.a.
1949	284.1	225.8	168.9	30.8	n.a.
1950	282.3	221.1	163.7	34.9	n.a.
1951	297.0	244.1	167.2	38.0	28.9
1952	302.5	239.1	170.3	38.2	30.6
1953	298.6	236.3	169.0	36.9	30.4
1954	316.3	248.1	167.8	38.9	41.6
1954 [a]	311.4	243.1	167.8	33.8	41.5
1955	314.3	245.1	167.7	34.1	n.a.
1956	323.9	252.7	169.7	35.6	47.4
1957	309.1	242.7	159.4	36.0	47.3
1958	306.0	237.3	150.8	36.5	50.0
1958 [b]	312.1	243.4	150.8	36.5	56.1
1959	313.2	249.1	149.7	38.3	61.1
1960	310.5	248.9	147.8	38.4	62.7
1961	306.9	245.3	143.5	36.3	65.5
1962	299.5	240.2	141.7	36.6	61.9
1963	299.6	238.6	138.4	36.4	63.8
1964	304.9	241.4	138.6	38.0	64.8
1965	299.8	237.5	136.1	35.9	65.5
1966	297.5	236.2	132.4	35.6	68.2
1967	305.0	244.0	133.0	37.0	74.0

Source: *U.S. Census of Manufactures, 1963*, Vol. II, Part 1. Meat Products, T. 1; *Annual Survey of Manufactures, 1964, 1965*, and *1966;* and *U.S. Census of Manufactures, 1967* (Preliminary Report).

[a] New definition. Beginning in 1954 processing carried on in wholesale branches of meat packing companies was excluded.

[b] New definition. Beginning in 1958 poultry canning was included.

Occupational Distribution

Table 6 compares the occupational distribution of the meat industry with that of manufacturing generally as reported by the 1960 Census of Population. In the semiskilled and unskilled occupational groups—operatives, service, and labor—meat products has a higher proportion of employees than all manufacturing. The converse is true in the higher rated jobs except for managers. Here the higher proportion in meat is probably attributable to the large number of small plants which require more factory management than do the smaller number of larger plants found in many other industries.

TABLE 6. *Meat Products and All Manufacturing*
Occupational Percentage Distribution of Employment
1960

| Occuptional Group | Percentage in Occupational Groups | |
	Meat Products	All Manufacturing
Professionals and technicians	1.8	7.5
Managers	5.6	5.1
Clerical workers	9.4	12.0
Sales workers	5.0	3.8
Craftsmen	7.6	19.6
Operatives	58.0	42.7
Service workers	1.9	1.6
Laborers	8.9	5.9
Occupation not reported	1.8	1.8
	100.0	100.0

Source: *U.S. Census of Population, 1960*, PC (2) 7C, *Occupation by Industry*,
          Table 2.

Table 7, utilizing data for 252 establishments for 1968, shows that the industry still employs the bulk of its personnel in low-rated jobs. Almost 80 percent are in blue collar categories and more than 60 percent are in semiskilled, unskilled, or service, with the number of laborers exceeding that of all white collar employees. Obviously the meat industry, much more than manufacturing generally, continues to have a large percentage of jobs which require relatively little or no skill, education, or training. A recent study supports the author's finding that the meat industry requires less schooling and length of training, on average, for its jobs than does manufacturing industry generally.[10] Meat industry employment has consisted of a relatively large number of low-skilled jobs since the last third of the nineteenth century, when the industry was converted into a highly rationalized, mass production activity. This low skill characteristic was a necessary condition for Negro entry to the industry during the first part of the twentieth century, because most black workers had little education or job training. But a large number of easy-to-learn jobs does not explain why Negroes were employed much earlier in meat packing than in other industries which also had many low-skilled occupations. Undesirable working conditions, strikebreaking, and other factors, to be discussed in the next two chapters, are better explanations of this occurrence.

TABLE 7. *Meat Industry, Employment By*
Occupational Group 252 Establishments
1968

Occupational Group	Number of Employees	Percent of Total
Officials and managers	8,445	7.5
Professionals	1,902	1.7
Technicians	1,110	1.0
Sales workers	4,809	4.2
Office and clerical workers	8,576	7.6
Total white collar	24,842	21.9
Craftsmen (skilled)	14,294	12.6
Operatives (semiskilled)	45,246	39.9
Laborers (unskilled)	26,752	23.6
Service workers	2,165	1.9
Total blue collar	88,457	78.1
Total	113,299	100.0

Source: Data in the author's possession.

Female Employment

Women comprised 27.5 percent of the meat industry's labor force in 1967 (Table 8), but more than 50 percent of the in-

---

[10] R.S. Eckhaus, "Economic Criteria for Education and Training," *Review of Economics and Statistics*, Vol. XLVI (May 1964), pp. 187-188.

dustry's females were employed in poultry plants, where they comprised 54.6 percent of the labor force as compared with 14.3 in meat packing and 29.4 in meat processing. The contraction of meat packing employment and concomitant expansion of poultry mean an increasing percentage of females will be employed in the industry. In the former sector, relatively highly paid Negro males have disproportionately suffered from the employment trend and industrial dispersion; in the latter, relatively low-paid Negro females are among the big gainers.

TABLE 8. *Meat Industry, Total and Female Employment*
By Standard Industrial Classification
1967

	Total Employees	Female Employees	Percent Female
Meat Products (SIC 201)	329,100	90,400	27.5
Meat Packing (SIC 2011)	187,800	26,900	14.3
Meat Processing (SIC 2013)	54,500	16,000	29.4
Poultry (SIC 2015)	86,800	47,400	54.6

Source: U.S. Bureau of Labor Statistics, *Employment and Earning Statistics for the United States, 1909-68*, Bulletin No. 1312-6, 1968, pp. 460-467.

Note: Bureau of Labor Statistics data are computed differently from Bureau of the Census data, so figures do not necessarily correspond with those in Table 2.

Earnings

Table 9 shows earnings in the meat industry and compares them with those in all manufacturing. It is clear that earnings in the meat industry, as a whole, are close to those received in other manufacturing industries. In 1968 production workers in the meat industry received an average of $2.99 per hour and $122.89 per week as compared with $3.01 and $122.51 in all manufacturing. The meat industry, moreover, pays substantially higher wages than other nondurable goods manufacturing.

As already noted, great disparities exist in earnings among the meat industry's segments. Meat packing plants averaged $3.45 per hour and $146.97 per week in 1968 as compared with $1.92 per hour and $74.11 per week in poultry plants. Moreover, even higher wages are found in some northern unionized packing facilities. The high wages in the meat packing plants are undoubtedly the twin function of the disagreeableness of the work and the consequent need to pay considerably more for work in order to attract labor, and the power and pressures of strong trade unionism. Over the years, this has meant high wages for work not highly rated as to skill. But this, in turn, has probably placed additional pressures on the industry's low profit margins and has accelerated automation, the substitution of equipment for labor, and the dispersal of the older center city facilities to smaller, more efficient plants near the sources of supply.

Meanwhile, the poultry industry has grown with its relatively low wages and heavily female labor force. Thus, the higher paid Negro (and, of course, white too) males of the center cities have lost jobs while lower paid Negro females have gained employment.

TABLE 9. *Average Weekly and Hourly Earnings*
Production Workers, Meat Industry and All Manufacturing
1968

	Average Weekly Earnings	Average Hourly Earnings
All Manufacturing	$122.51	$3.01
Durable goods	132.07	3.19
Nondurable goods	109.05	2.74
Meat Products (SIC 201)	122.89	2.99
Meat packing (SIC 2011)	146.97	3.45
Meat processing (SIC 2013)	131.38	3.22
Poultry (SIC 2015)	74.11	1.92

Source: *Employment and Earnings*, Vol. 15 (March 1969), Table C-2.

Unionization

Despite repeated attempts at organization, and some temporary success, unions were not able to gain a foothold before the late 1930's. The Amalgamated Meat Cutters and Butcher Workmen of North America, the American Federation of Labor affiliate having prime jurisdiction in the industry, survived prior to that time primarily because of its success in organizing retail butchers. During the 1930's and 1940's, however, most major meat packing plants were unionized either by the Amalgamated, or by a new CIO rival, the United Packinghouse Workers of America (UPWA).

Thanks no little to its more equalitarian policies, and consequent heavy Negro worker support, the latter was more successful in the major packing centers, but the Amalgamated remained the larger union overall. A third union, the National Brotherhood of Packinghouse Workers, which grew out of an employer representation plan, obtained bargaining rights at some Swift plants.

The concentration of the Packinghouse Workers' membership in the major packing centers led to a decline in its membership as these plants were closed. In 1968, after several years of cooperation in collective bargaining and policies pertaining to readjustments pursuant to plant closings, the two major unions merged, with the Amalgamated the surviving organization.

The poultry sector is much less unionized than is meat packing or meat processing. Many poultry plants are in small southern towns where unionization is much less common than elsewhere in the country.

Initially the Amalgamated was craft oriented and unenthusiastic about attempts to unionize black workers, who in turn were often brought in as strikebreakers. The need to unionize all employees forced it to alter its policies; and the strong equalitarian bent of the Packinghouse Workers contributed further to moving the Amalgamated toward a policy of equality. Because of the significance of union relations and unionism in determining the position of Negroes in the industry, union policy will be given considerable attention in the following chapters.

CHAPTER III.

Early Turbulence: The Years to World War I

Growth and change in the meat industry during the last part of the nineteenth century created many unskilled, physically demanding jobs. Recent immigrants were the primary source of labor for these jobs, but as workers' attempts to unionize increased, meat packers discovered that black workers provided an alternative source of labor. This circumstance of the initial Negro entry into meat industry employment—strikebreaking—had a far-reaching impact on relations between whites and blacks in meat packing cities.

THE EARLY NEED FOR UNSKILLED LABOR

The meat industry in the United States did not employ large numbers of workers until the last quarter of the nineteenth century. In that period, the extension of railroads and, especially, the development of refrigeration processes and the refrigerated railroad car brought about a rapid expansion of the industry; between 1870 and 1900 employment increased from 10,000 to 70,000.[11] At the turn of the century the activity of the industry consisted almost entirely of meat packing—the conversion of livestock into fresh cuts of meat. Intensive processing of meat, including poultry, did not become a major part of the industry until much later.

As employment in meat packing expanded, the nature of work in the industry changed drastically. The preparation of meat cuts from livestock became highly rationalized in the last two decades of the nineteenth century. The rationalization was characterized especially by the use of conveyors that moved animal carcasses through many stages of disassembly and processing. Highly specialized tasks were performed by many workers at each of these stages. Most jobs in meat packing now became easy to learn even if arduous to perform. Although a number

[11] Alma Herbst, *The Negro in the Slaughtering and Meat Packing Industry in Chicago* (New York: Houghton Mifflin Co., 1932), p. 155.

of skilled cutting jobs were retained by the improved methods, many other tasks which skilled men had previously performed as part of the complete craft of butchering could now be assigned to unskilled workers.[12]

The reductions which occurred in the skills required for work in meat packing could be turned to the advantage of employers in the industry only if a plentiful supply of unskilled labor was available. Workers who had skills and a moderate amount of formal education would not work in meat packing at common labor wages. For most persons who had alternative job opportunities, very high wages indeed would have been required to attract them to meat packing, with its unpleasant, dangerous work and seasonal insecurity of employment. At the time, however, many immigrants to the country did not possess skills which provided entry to desirable jobs and these newcomers became a satisfactory source of labor supply to the meat packing industry. From the initial development of the industry until World War II, immigrants filled most of the low-skilled jobs.

At the turn of the century, meat packing employers had no need for Negro workers except to keep unions in check. Negroes obtained few of the new jobs which were added in the industry between 1870 and the end of the century. Most meat packing at that time was done in the North and few Negroes had yet migrated to that part of the country. Since the low-skilled jobs in the major stockyards, where most meat packing was carried out, were easily filled from the ranks of immigrants, there was no need to turn to the Negro who was still not considered for industrial activity by most white Americans. The jobs went instead, first, to the Irish, German, and English immigrants and, in the last two decades of the century, to newcomers from eastern Europe in accord with changes which took place in the ethnic composition of immigration to the United States.

In 1881, as in the next 70 years, Chicago was the meat packing center of the country. Of 6,500 Negroes who were then living in the city (according to the Census of 1880), only two were employed in the meat industry. More Negroes were employed in the border state packing centers of St. Louis and Kansas City and in plants serving local markets in the South, but the total

_____

[12] John R. Commons, "Labor Conditions in Meat Packing and the Recent Strike," *Quarterly Journal of Economics*, Vol. XIX (November 1904), p. 3; David Brody, *The Butcher Workmen* (Cambridge: Harvard University Press, 1964), pp. 3-9; Herbst, *op. cit.*, pp. 6-9.

number of Negroes in the industry must have been very small. The relative unimportance of Negro workers may be inferred from the lack of their mention in connection with early meat industry strikes such as that of October 1886 over hours of work.[13] Eleven years later, it was to be a different story, and a pattern was established for Negro entry into the industry.

The 1894 Strike

In 1894 the newly formed butchers' union, which was affiliated with the then declining Knights of Labor, called a strike in the Chicago Union Stock Yards with the ostensible purpose of expressing sympathy for Eugene V. Debs' American Railway Union which was engaged in a bitter dispute with the Pullman company. This ill-timed strike may have been ideologically satisfying, but it was certainly strategically disastrous for the growth of unionization in the industry. Employees who left their jobs were easily replaced from among the thousands of unemployed workers who crowded the yards, anxious to take any job they could get. Although employers first hired recent immigrants from eastern Europe to replace the strikers, Negroes, too, were soon used in that capacity. Many Negro laborers living in Chicago were aware that a provision in the constitution of the American Railway Union, which professed to be open to all railroad workers, barred them from membership, as did nearly all other railroad unions. Furthermore, jobs as good as those in meat packing had rarely been open to them—in stock yards or in other industries prior to the strike. The fact that these jobs became available because white workers were striking in support of a labor union in another industry was not sufficient reason to keep black workers from accepting them, particularly when the union being supported discriminated against black people.

Violence, fanned by racial sentiments, was part of the strike of 1894. Strikers sought vengeance against those who were taking their jobs, and Negroes were most frequently the targets of their emotions even though the majority of the strikebreakers were white. An effigy of a Negro was hung from a telephone pole near the entrance to the Union Stock Yards; and a number of Negro workers were badly beaten. But most significant of all, the events of that labor dispute engendered great lasting bitterness toward the Negro race. Many white workers now saw

[13] Herbst, *op. cit.*, pp. 15-17.

Negroes as a threat to their efforts to unionize and improve the generally miserable working conditions which prevailed in the Chicago yards. Similar feelings were also directed at some immigrant ethnic groups which had participated in breaking the strike, but the Negro, because of his color, attracted more than his share of hostility.

After the conclusion of the strike most Negro workers were discharged. The experience gained, however, was exploited by the packers. By employing a relatively small number of Negroes after 1894,

> the packers profited on two accounts; first, they tapped an almost inexhaustible supply of cheap labor; second, they secured thereby a labor force offering even greater resistance to unionization, through racial antagonism, than that supplied by the immigrant through language handicap and nationality hatreds.[14]

Now the context within which black workers were to enter the meat industry, in many smaller packing centers as well as in Chicago, was established; it was that of employer efforts to keep trade unionism out of their establishments. The antiunion motivation was to dominate the employment of Negroes in meat packing until World War I and even then, when labor shortages became the major reason for hiring Negroes, employer opposition to unions remained an important secondary factor. As we shall see, the resentment to the Negro engendered in white workers by this employer policy carried over into the residential communities in which packinghouse workers lived.

The 1904 Strike

The black worker next played a prominent role in the meat packing industry during the labor dispute of 1904. The strike of that year followed organizing efforts of the newly formed Amalgamated Meat Cutters and Butcher Workmen of North America—the union which was to dominate attempts to organize the meat industry until the 1930's. Although principally a union of skilled butchers, the Amalgamated from its beginning attempted, with varying degrees of enthusiasm, to organize less skilled workers. A study by the U.S. Bureau of Labor in 1905 asserted that the union "was the only Americanizing influence"

---

[14] *Ibid.*, pp. 19-20.

in the stockyards for the Poles, Lithuanians and Slavs.[15] The union solicited Negro membership from the beginning, and at least a few of the 500 Negroes who worked in the Chicago stockyards did join prior to the strike of 1904.[16]

The strike was called to support Amalgamated demands for a minimum wage of 18 cents an hour for unskilled workers and for geographic uniformity of pay scales. The packers rejected these demands, confident that prevailing labor market conditions would force the union to back down on its demands. The packers contended that even at the prevailing rate of 16.5 cents an hour, 3,000 to 5,000 transient laborers sought work each morning in the Union Stock Yards, and that jobs were available for less than one-tenth of them.[17]

As ten years earlier, strikebreakers from many ethnic groups were employed in the Chicago yards. This time Negroes were present in larger numbers than previously and immediately became the object of the strikers' passions.

> As the presence of an increasing number of immigrants and Negroes in the yards indicated the success of the packers in resuming operations, racial antipathies and hatreds were kindled. To the striking union men no scabs were as loathsome as the Negroes who took their jobs. Easily distinguishable, they were conspicuous among the strikebreakers. They were jeered if they emerged from the plants under police escort; chased and attacked if alone. Pistol shots invariably brought the assaults to a close.[18]

An estimated 2,000 Negroes were hired during the seven-week strike. Although the first Negroes employed were recruited not far from the yards, the packers soon began to import workers into the city. ". . . [T]rainloads of several hundred Negroes, accompanied by officers of the law, arrived daily." Perlman and Taft estimated that 1,400 workers, mostly Negroes, were brought in from the South. In addition to the importation of Negroes, at least one train of several hundred immigrants traveled di-

---

[15] U.S. Bureau of Labor, *Influence of Trade Unions on Immigrants,* Bulletin No. 56 (Washington: Government Printing Office, 1905), p. 4.

[16] Sterling Spero and Abram Harris, *The Black Worker* (New York: Columbia University Press, 1931), p. 266; Herbst, *op. cit.,* p. 22.

[17] Commons, *op. cit.,* p. 26.

[18] Herbst, *op. cit.,* pp. 24-25.

rectly from the Ellis Island port of entry to the Chicago stock-yards. According to Herbst, 25 percent of the strikebreakers, including many Negroes, were lodged in the packing houses for three weeks.[19]

This meat packing strike provided one of the first opportunities for black workers in the North to break into manufacturing jobs. In 1900, most Negroes in Chicago were employed as service workers; less than 10 percent of Negro employment was in manufacturing industries. Nevertheless, the packers recruited Negroes from the South during the strike, as well as from Chicago's South Side. Some of the black workers brought from the South refused to work once they learned the circumstances of their job opportunities; most, however, knew nothing about unions or strikes, or if they did, grasped the employment opportunity.[20]

The use of strikebreakers, black and white, had impacts which spilled out of the Union Stock Yards to the larger community. The Ashland Avenue Business Men's Association, composed of businessmen of the stockyards district, protested to the mayor of Chicago about the importation of laborers, calling them "a menace to Chicago" and "future paupers."[21] Of course, the striking workers used much harsher language in condemning the strikebreakers. As the packers gradually resumed operations, the strikers began attacking those who worked wherever they could. Almost all of the victims of stonings and beatings were Negroes.[22]

Nevertheless, the strikebreaking was successful and the packers were able to resume full operations. An exaggeration of the role played by Negroes in its defeat led union officials to a rather ominous perception of future race relations in the industry:

> Without the colored men and women now employed in the plants the companies would not be able to operate. The employers have been unable to hire white men. If the pres-

---

[19] Allan H. Spear, *Black Chicago* (Chicago: University of Chicago Press, 1967), p. 38; Herbst, *op. cit.*, pp. 24-25; Selig Perlman and Philip Taft, *History of Labor in the United States, 1896-1932*, Vol. IV, *Labor Movements* (New York: Macmillan Co., 1935), p. 120; Spero and Harris, *op. cit.*, p. 266.

[20] Spear, *op. cit.*, p. 30; Spero and Harris, *op. cit.*, p. 267.

[21] Harry Rosenberg, "Packing Industry and the Stockyards," unpublished memorandum in Mary McDowell papers, Chicago Historical Society, n.d.

[22] Spear, *op. cit.*, p. 37.

ent system is kept up, race hatred will be stirred up and trouble may follow.[23]

Less than one year later, a race riot occurred in Chicago during which several people were killed and many others injured. The immediate cause of the violence was the use of Negroes to break a teamster strike. It is a reasonable speculation that the events in meat packing of the preceding year added to the racial antagonisms which were violently expressed in the riot.

Employment After the Strike of 1904

At the end of the strike of 1904, most Negroes lost their jobs in the meat packing industry, either because they were discharged by the employers or because they were intimidated into leaving by returning strikers. "The colored deserters were herded into special trains which carried them to the Black Belt of Chicago. The packers preferred white laborers and hired them to replace the Negroes whose services as strikebreakers were no longer required." [24]

After its defeat, the Amalgamated almost disappeared from the meat packing centers in Chicago and elsewhere. The necessity of organizing Negroes had been demonstrated for the second time to a meat packing union. It was to be vividly demonstrated again, during the labor strife of World War I and the early postwar years.

Black workers during the strike had once again shown both their ability to perform meat packing jobs and their willingness to do so during strikes called by organized labor. These attributes, however, did not provide them with gains in employment or job advancement as long as the union was no threat to employers. By 1910, less than 400 Negroes were employed in Chicago meat packing, according to the census of that year.

Negro experiences in meat packing can be much better described for Chicago than for other industry locations. Much has been written about meat packing in Chicago because it was for so many years the center of the industry and its labor rela-

---

[23] Herbst, *op. cit.*, p. 26, quoted from the *Chicago Daily Tribune*, August 24, 1904, p. 3. The statement was given by John Fitzpatrick, who was then assigned by the Chicago Federation of Labor to head organizing efforts in the Union Stock Yards and who later became president of the Chicago Federation of Labor.

[24] Herbst, *op. cit.*, p. 27.

tions were so often traumatic. The federal census of population for 1910, however, makes it clear that Chicago lagged behind much of the rest of the industry in admitting Negroes to employment. In 1910, 5,800 black workers, about 6 percent of total employment, were working in the meat industry; [25] according to the figure previously given, less than 10 percent of them worked in Chicago. Two hundred or more Negroes were employed in each of the following meat packing centers in 1910: East St. Louis, St. Louis, Greater Kansas City (Kansas City, Kansas, and Kansas City, Missouri), and Omaha.[26] Texas employed more Negroes in the industry than any other state in 1910—the census counted over 800, in unskilled jobs alone.[27]

Information on the circumstances of Negro entry into meat industry centers other than Chicago is not readily available. Strikebreaking probably played some part in the secondary locations as well as in Chicago—Perlman and Taft state that in the strike of 1904, 150 Negroes were brought to St. Joseph, Missouri, to replace striking workers, though the strikers persuaded half of them not to work. Strike violence, which was very probably associated at least in part with the use of Negroes as strikebreakers, also erupted in 1904 at Sioux City, Omaha, Kansas City, and Fort Worth.[28] It is likely, however, that in the smaller centers the need to augment the white labor supply was a more important factor than combating unions, as was the case in Chicago. Organized labor was stronger and organizing efforts had been more successful in Chicago than in the smaller

----

[25] *U.S. Census of Population, 1910*, Vol. IV, *Occupation Statistics*, Table VII. Paul S. Taylor, in his *Mexican Labor in the United States, Chicago and the Calumet Region* (Berkeley: University of California Press, 1928), p. 45, suggested that the census figures for Negro meat packing employment in Chicago in 1910 and 1920 were too low because U. S. Immigration Commission reports for these years showed substantially larger numbers of Negroes as employed in this industry in Chicago. However, Taylor overlooked the census categories of "stockyard laborers" and "butchers," and, in fact, many persons reporting these occupations in the censuses for 1910 and 1920 were employed in Union Stock Yards meat packing firms (see Appendix Table A-1). When these two occupational groups are included, the census figures on Negroes working in meat packing are approximately the same as those reported by the Immigration Service.

[26] *U.S. Census, 1910*, Table VII; inferred from state information in this table.

[27] *Ibid.* This source did not enumerate Negro "operatives" in Texas meat packing for 1910.

[28] Perlman and Taft, *op. cit.*, p. 121.

midwestern cities. Negroes living in the South were closer to the Missouri, southern Illinois, and Kansas meat packing cities; the pattern of migration brought them into the labor supply of those cities before much movement to Chicago had taken place. Finally, the supply of immigrant labor relative to the size of the labor force was probably larger for Chicago than for the other cities; and, therefore, Negro job opportunities may have been better in the other cities.

Still, it was strikebreaking that afforded black workers their first opportunity to break into the meat industry in significant numbers. As long as labor relations were peaceful, the packers had little need for Negroes. But in labor disputes, Negroes, along with unemployed immigrants, were a useful source of replacements for striking workers.

THE WORLD WAR I YEARS

Negro employment in the meat industry increased substantially between 1910 and 1920, with almost all of the gains concentrated in the last four years of the decade. These employment gains could not have occurred without migration of black people to the metropolitan centers of the industry. In turn, the increases in Negro employment directly affected labor relations and community race relations in meat packing centers, sometimes with tragic results.

Negro Migration

Several events led up to the massive migration of Negroes which occurred in the United States after 1916. Between 1913 and 1916, thousands of southern black belt Negroes lost their livelihoods through a series of agriculture disasters. As a result of World War I, immigration to the United States dropped from 1,220,000 in 1914 to 330,000 in 1915. In 1916, the nation's economy began to expand and, with the decline in immigration, jobs became available in northern industry. It was then that Negroes began to migrate from the South in large numbers. The meat packing centers, along with northern industrial cities generally, were the destinations of many of these migrants. Between 1910 and 1920, Chicago's Negro population increased by more than that of any other city in the country—from 44,000 to 109,000. The Negro population of East St. Louis, another leading center of the meat packing industry, grew almost as rapidly: from 5,900 in 1910 to 10,600 in 1918. Other important locations of the industry—Indianapolis, St. Louis, Omaha, Kansas City, and several smaller cities—also received large numbers of Negro migrants.[29]

Much of the Negro migration took place in the last four years of the decade. Spear estimated that 50,000 Negroes arrived in Chicago between 1916 and 1920. Similarly, most of the black migrants to East St. Louis arrived after 1916.[30]

Labor agents played a significant role in initiating the movement to the North, offering "free transportation plus the prospect of high wages to any laborer who agreed to migrate." [31]

The meat packing firms of the North were well aware of the benefits of Negro migration. The packers opposed policies designed to slow the migration when these were proposed by organized labor and civic groups; they also utilized labor agents upon occasion. The role of the labor agent, however, was chiefly one of timing—initiating the movement at the moment most advantageous for large employers in the North. After the migration had begun there was no further need for labor agents.[32]

In Chicago, the Negro newspaper, *The Defender*—widely read in the South—encouraged migration not only for economic gain, but also for human dignity. It urged Negroes to leave the place where they did not have "the standing of a man and a citizen in the community." *The Defender* set May 15, 1917, as the date for the "Great Northern Drive." It supplemented its Help Wanted columns with news headlines, such as "More Positions Open Than Men For Them." [33]

But the most important force behind the migration was the personal message from friends or relatives who had already gone North. A Negro woman who had recently arrived in Chicago wrote to a friend in the South:

> I am well and thankful to say I am doing well. I work in
> Swifts packing Co., in the sausage department. . . . We

---

[29] Spear, *op. cit.*, pp. 132, 140; Elliott M. Rudwick, *Race Riot at East St. Louis* (Carbondale: Southern Illinois University Press, 1964), p. 165.

[30] Spear, *op. cit.*, p. 140; Rudwick, *op. cit.*, p. 165.

[31] Spear, *op. cit.*, p. 133.

[32] Arvarh E. Strickland, *History of the Chicago Urban League* (Urbana: University of Illinois Press, 1966), p. 58; Rudwick, *op. cit.*, pp. 21-22.

[33] Spear, *op. cit.*, p. 134.

get $1.50 a day. . . . Tell your husband work is plentiful here and he wont have to loaf if he want to work.[34]

This letter is representative. Meat packing was the leading industry of employment for Negro males who migrated to Chicago during the era of World War I,[35] and this was probably also true in East St. Louis, Kansas City, Indianapolis, and Omaha.

Employment Changes, 1910-1920

The meat industry greatly increased its employment of black workers during World War I. In 1910, the population census reported that 5,800 Negroes were employed in the industry; by 1920 the number had risen to over 28,000. (Table 10.) The latter figure includes unskilled and semiskilled workers (laborers and operatives, respectively) only, but it is comparable to the 1910 figure because in that year all but approximately 60 Negroes in meat packing were working in these categories. In relative terms, the increase was from 9 to 21 percent of low-skilled (laborer and operative) employment and from 6 to an estimated 15 percent of all employment. The Negro shares of employment in 1917 and 1918 had been substantially larger— perhaps as large as one-third of the low-skilled category. Black workers were clearly an essential part of the wartime work force in meat packing.

The greatest increases in Negro employment took place in the packing centers of states which bordered on former slave states. Illinois led all other states with a twelve-fold increase, from 850 in 1910 to 10,000 in 1920. Meat packing employment of Negroes in Missouri (Kansas City, St. Louis, St. Joseph) rose from 600 in 1910 to almost 5,000 10 years later. In St. Louis, Negroes comprised 60 percent of all low-skilled meat packing employees by 1920. In Kansas (Kansas City and Wichita), the increase in Negro workers was from 800 to 2,600; in Indiana (Indianapolis), it was from less than 100 to 1,200.[36]

---

[34] *Ibid.*

[35] Chicago Commission on Race Relations, *The Negro in Chicago* (Chicago: The Commission, 1922), pp. 95, 166-168.

[36] Computed from data in *U.S. Census of Population, 1910*, Vol. IV; *1920*, Vol. IV. "Stockyard laborers" are included in the Illinois figures. (See also Appendix Table A-1.)

TABLE 10. *Meat Industry*
Total and Negro Employment, 1910-1960

	Total	Negro	Percent Negro
1910	94,400	5,800	6.2
1920	132,400[a]	28,300[a]	21.4[a]
	197,900[b]	30,000[b]	15.2[b]
1930	173,600	20,400	11.8
1940	210,100	16,200	7.7
1950	273,900	39,100	14.3
1960	318,000	43,900	13.8

Source: *U.S. Census of Population:*

    1920, Vol. IV, *Occupations*, Tables 6, 10.
    1930, Vol. IV, *Occupations—General Report*, Table 1.
    1940, Vol. III, *The Labor Force*, Part 1, Table 76.
    1950, Vol. II, *Characteristics of the Population*, Part 1, Table 133.
    1960, PC(1) D, *Detailed Characteristics*, Part 1, Table 213.

Note: See Appendix Table A-1 for an explanation of the derivation of this table.

[a] Operatives and laborers.

[b] Estimate for all occupations.

The use of Negroes to fill labor requirements in meat packing during World War I was not, however, confined to the border states. By 1920, Negroes had also entered the industry in more northerly centers; Nebraska (principally Omaha) employed 1,500, Iowa 600, and Minnesota 300. Meat packing was certainly the principal attraction for the Negro migration to Omaha which occurred at this time; it was probably also instrumental in drawing Negroes to Cedar Rapids, Des Moines, Sioux City, and Waterloo, Iowa, and St. Paul, Minnesota.

Chicago, in World War I as earlier, was by far the leading meat packing center in the country, employing more than one-fourth of all workers in the industry. Although prior to World War I, Chicago employed fewer Negroes in meat packing than some of the other centers of the industry, this changed quickly during the war and by 1920, 8,600 blacks worked in the industry in Chicago. Almost one-third of all Negro packinghouse workers were now concentrated in that city. Earlier, in 1917 and 1918, 12,000 to 15,000 Negroes were employed in the Chicago stockyards. Herbst estimated that in a few plants the wartime employment of Negroes reached 60 to 70 percent.[37]

Almost all of the war decade increase in Negro employment occurred after 1916. The data in Table 11, based upon employment records of one large Chicago packing firm, illustrate both the expansion in total employment and the rise in the comparative number of Negro workers.

TABLE 11. *Meat Industry*
Total and Negro Employment
One Major Chicago Packing Company, January 1916-
December 1918

	Total Employment	Negro Employment	Percent Negro
January 1916	8,361	311	3.7
July 1916	8,062	733	9.1
January 1917	10,255	1,657	16.2
July 1917	10,679	2,278	21.3
January 1918	13,878	3,069	22.1
July 1918	15,336	2,323	15.1
December 1918	17,434	3,621	20.8

Source: George E. Haynes, *The Negro at Work During the World War and During Reconstruction*, U.S. Department of Labor, Division of Negro Economics (Washington: Government Printing Office, 1921), pp. 54-55.

By 1920, the meat industry had become a very important source of employment opportunities for the black populations of several northern cities. In Chicago, this industry employed more than one-half of all Negro men who held jobs in manufacturing. Steel, the next largest employer of Negroes, had 1,900—less than one-fourth the number in the meat industry. In Omaha and Kansas City, Kansas, as well, the meat industry employed more than one-half of all Negroes who were in manufacturing, and 30 to 40 percent, respectively, of all male Negro workers.[38] But even these figures do not tell the full story, for they do not include the many Negroes who worked in meat packing and then

---

[37] Herbst, *op. cit.*, pp. xxii, 30; Spero and Harris, *op. cit.*, p. 271.

[38] *U.S. Census of Population, 1920*, Vol. IV. The Chicago figures are based on comparisons which include "stockyard laborers." (See Appendix Table A-1.)

moved on to other jobs in these cities. At the end of World War I, it is probable that most adult male Negroes in Chicago, and perhaps in a few other cities, had working experience in a meat packing establishment.

The major reason for the increased use of black workers throughout the meat industry was the wartime labor shortage. With the supply of immigrant labor cut off by the war, the major packers were forced to turn to Negroes for cheap labor; many whites who, before the war, would have accepted employment in meat packing now had job opportunities in more desirable industries. The lack of education and job skills of Negro workers was no handicap to their employment in meat packing because the industry had so many low-skilled jobs. The undesirable working conditions in meat establishments did not stop Negroes from taking jobs in them—many preferred these working conditions to bare subsistence in the South.

NEGROES AND MEAT PACKING UNIONS, 1916-1921

Although the packers' major motivation for hiring Negroes during the period of World War I was the meeting of labor requirements, they also realized that black workers would be an asset in the battle against militant trade unionism. The reluctance of Negroes to join unions and their willingness to work during strikes had been amply demonstrated in the Chicago meat industry. Following the defeat of the Amalgamated in the 1904 strike, a defeat which was ensured by the presence of Negro strikebreakers, unionism in the industry did not revive until 1916.

Booming business conditions brought about by the war stirred the Amalgamated to undertake heavy organizing activities in 1917. This time, its leaders were determined to persuade Negroes to become union members, and important measures, such as the use of Negro organizers, were taken to accommodate the special interests of black workers. These efforts, however, were often futile in the face of Negro antipathy toward unions, their lack of knowledge of union goals, and white worker antagonism toward the blacks.[39]

In order to coordinate organization efforts, a Stock Yards Labor Council, with William Z. Foster as secretary, was formed

---

[39] Herbst, *op. cit.*, pp. 28-31; Chicago Commission on Race Relations, *op. cit.*, pp. 428-429 (testimony of W.Z. Foster); W.Z. Foster, *The Great Steel Strike* (New York: B.W. Huebsch, 1920), pp. 211-212.

in 1917, under the jurisdiction of the Chicago Federation of Labor. Approximately 20 unions, including the Amalgamated, which was by far the largest organization, were affiliated with the Council; most of these were skilled craft groups. Only a few of the unions, including the Amalgamated, admitted Negroes to membership. Since there was now a very large number of Negroes in the Chicago yards, "the number increasing in direct ratio to the success of the unions in organizing the white laborers," [40] it was evident that "the Negro problem" had to be dealt with if unionism was to achieve any success. In short, the problem was that black workers had to be organized, but many white workers with strong racial prejudices did not want union "brotherhood" with their colored coworkers. The dilemma was presented to Samuel Gompers, President of the American Federation of Labor, for his recommendation. He suggested the formation of a separate Amalgamated local for Negroes, which would take in all Negroes in the yards, whatever their job. Two colored organizers were hired and Local 651 of the Amalgamated was formed. It signed up most of the black workers who did join unions in the Chicago yards, thus enabling the unions of skilled workers to remain all white. Some early successes were obtained in organizing Negroes, but these gains were often temporary, and, on the whole, the success of the meat packing unions with Negroes was limited—in the Chicago yards, never more than 15 percent were organized.[41]

Although the effort to organize Negroes appears to have been sincere, it probably appeared more calculating than altruistic to black workers. Many were aware of the fact that, generally, unions did not admit Negroes to membership. Even more realized that Negroes rarely were advanced above semiskilled positions in meat packing and that unions had done nothing to change the practice. Certainly, all were aware of the antagonistic feelings harbored by many white workers toward members of their race.

During the war and immediately after it, employers in the meat industry continually increased their employment of Negroes, partially because of their belief that unions could not capture the support of black workers. In an apparent response to a recommendation from the president of Swift and Company, the

---

[40] Herbst, *op. cit.*, p. 30.

[41] Brody, *op. cit.*, p. 86; Herbst, *op. cit.*, Chapter 3; Spero and Harris, *op. cit.*, p. 271.

manager of Swift's Denver plant sent a reply stating his agreement to "increase the percentage of colored help in the plant with the intention of getting it to 15 percent or higher as soon as we possibly can." [42] The packers were aided in their anti-union efforts by a Negro promoter, Richard Parker, who claimed that he had brought more Negroes from the South than any other person in Chicago. Parker ran an employment agency, a newspaper, and a quiescent labor organization—the American Unity Labor Union. He advertised the latter as the only union in the stockyards having a bona fide interest in the Negro worker, and he warned that Negroes would lose their jobs if they joined other unions. Parker has been called an agent of the packers, although a direct connection has never been proved. The Chicago packers also made financial efforts to obtain good relationships with institutions in the black community such as the YMCA and the churches. Finally, as a direct means of attacking unions, many white union members were discharged during the wartime organizing drives and not infrequently replaced with Negroes. [43]

The East St. Louis Strike

Failure to organize Negroes led to disastrous consequences for meat packing unions. In the summer of 1916, for example, the Amalgamated struck the Armour, Swift, and Morris firms in East St. Louis. Meat packing was the leading industry in that small industrial city, employing 4,000 workers, about 40 percent of whom were black. The strike was quickly broken and union leaders blamed their defeat on the importation of Negroes, asserting that 800 to 1,500 had been brought in to break the strike. This was probably an exaggeration of the true number; however, use of strikebreakers did contribute significantly to the union's defeat. The managers of the Armour and Swift plants each acknowledged in Congressional hearings they had imported between 40 and 60 southern Negroes. Following the strike, labor relations in East St. Louis meat packing continued to be characterized by bitterness and strife. Union officials asserted that the refusal of the companies to reemploy union lead-

---

[42] Spero and Harris, *op. cit.*, p. 269; Herbst, *op. cit.*, p. 34.

[43] Chicago Commission on Race Relations, *op. cit.*, p. 423; Spear, *op. cit.*, p. 162; Herbst, *op. cit.*, pp. 34-36; Spero and Harris, *op. cit.*, p. 273.

ers was in violation of the agreement which had ended the strike.[44]

When employment in the industry expanded in 1917, the Negro proportion of the work force in East St. Louis was kept at 40 percent.

> Management had two reasons for maintaining the consistently large Negro proportions: race differences among the employees decreased the possibility of unionization, and Negroes did not object to performing low-paying, dirty, unpleasant tasks involved in fertilizer manufacturing and hog killing.[45]

The Negro's acquiescence to the unpleasant jobs in the industry was undoubtedly based on lack of better alternatives; his opportunities for more desirable industrial jobs was severely limited.

The Amalgamated in East St. Louis collapsed in 1917 as membership fell to 30 from 1,500 the previous year. Of primary importance to this collapse was the ability of employers to use as a club the threat of employing more Negroes, who by now were arriving in large numbers from the South. Labor officials realized that under those circumstances another strike was out of the question. These officials reacted bitterly to their frustration by using the race issue as the focal point of attacks upon the companies. In the spring of 1917, the local Amalgamated newspaper carried stories claiming that the meat packers had brought thousands of Negroes to the city, that three-fourths of the packinghouse workers were Negro, and that employers in the city planned to import another 10,000 to 15,000 in order to make East St. Louis "a Negro town." There was little foundation in fact for these claims. They were, however, believed by many white residents of the city, and led a few months later, as will be described below, to one of the worst race riots in United States history.[46]

---

[44] U.S. Department of Labor, *Negro Migration in 1916-17* (Washington: Government Printing Office, 1919), pp. 130-131; Rudwick, *op. cit.*, p. 20.

[45] Rudwick, *op. cit.*, p. 22.

[46] *Ibid.*, pp. 22-33.

The Chicago Strike

A more important test for meat packing unions occurred in Chicago and, to a lesser extent, in other meat packing centers. The limited success of the stockyard labor unions in organizing Negroes during the war did not have adverse consequences until 1921. This was largely because in late 1917, to avert a threatened strike, President Wilson's wartime Mediation Commission appointed Judge Samuel S. Alschuler of the Circuit Court of Appeals as arbitrator for the industry. Alschuler held this position until September 1921, during which time strikes did not occur and substantial improvements in working conditions were obtained by the workers.

By 1921, however, relations between Negroes and the stockyard unions had markedly deteriorated, principally as a result of the Chicago race riot of 1919, to be discussed later. During that event, union leaders had attempted to act as peacemakers, but some violence did occur in and near the yards, with meat packing workers, both white and black, as the victims. Perhaps an even greater strain on race relations was a fire which occurred during the riot and burned 49 homes in white neighborhoods immediately west of the Union Stock Yards. Although the arsonists were never caught, many whites believed that Negroes had set the fires.

When the agreement under which Judge Alschuler had served as arbitrator for the meat industry was terminated in September 1921, a depression was in full progress. The packers immediately prepared to reduce wages, operating through employee representation groups which they had recently established. The Amalgamated demanded continuation of the current wage scale, but the packers refused to negotiate with them. The Amalgamated and other unions affiliated with the Stock Yards Labor Council struck on December 5th. This strike, which affected other meat centers as well as Chicago, lasted for almost two months and ended in complete defeat for the unions.[47]

Some Negroes who were employed in the Chicago yards prior to the strike supported it, but most probably did not. Black workers were recruited both locally and from the South to break the strike. They were used for this purpose not only in Chicago,

---

[47] Brody, *op. cit.*, Chapter 5; Herbst, *op. cit.*, Chapter 3.

but also in St. Louis, Kansas City, Omaha, St. Paul, and other meat packing centers.[48]

The goodwill which the packers had previously purchased within parts of Chicago's black community now served them well. On the Sunday immediately preceding the 1921 strike, ministers in many of Chicago's Negro churches read messages from the packers urging workmen to disregard the strike order. The Urban League of Chicago supplied the packers with 450 workers during the strike, although it refused to recruit for firms which had not previously hired Negroes. The Chicago League, since its formation in 1916, had striven to cooperate with both employers and organized labor. This could not always be done, however, and when forced to choose, the League went with the employers—they, not the unions, had the jobs. The dependence of the League upon wealthy whites for financial support also may have influenced its actions during the strike.[49]

Why Black Workers Did Not Support the Unions

By 1921, Negroes had a sizeable stake in wages and working conditions in the meat industry. They held about 20 percent of the jobs in the entire industry and even larger proportions in some local plants. Yet, according to all reports of the period, black workers then employed in the industry gave only weak support to the strike and others became strikebreakers. How can these facts be explained?

The most thorough investigation of these events, at least for the Chicago meat industry, was done by Alma Herbst, who suggests several explanations.[50] First, there was the low economic condition of Negroes:

> . . . in the seventeen years between 1904 and 1921, conditions in meat packing had changed so that the Negro was faced with a choice of giving allegiance to the packers or the worker organizations. In the face of an emergency which involved a decision as unequivocal as this the Negro faltered only momentarily. To him the choice was between a job and no job; economic necessity was so great that primary needs determined his fealty. He sought favor and

---

[48] Spero and Harris, *op. cit.*, p. 281; Herbst, *op. cit.*, p. 65.

[49] Spear, *op. cit.*, p. 173; Strickland, *op. cit.*, p. 73.

[50] Herbst, *op. cit.*, pp. 59-65.

protection where they were to be found; lip service to the union was abandoned.[51]

Second, the southern Negro was inclined by his experience to be grateful for the employer's paternalism and to look upon him as providing a source of livelihood. In 1918 and 1919, the packers had given many jobs to Negroes who had never known economic security. Third, Negroes realized that, other things being equal, most employers preferred white workers.

> In the yards, the colored man had sensed the fact that as a colored trade-unionist, his position was anomalous and precarious; if forced to recognize and to employ members of labor organizations, the employers would quickly dispense with as great a number of colored unionists as the available labor supply would permit.[52]

Fourth, most Negroes realized at least vaguely that trade unions generally had not been hospitable to members of their race. Where Negroes had succeeded in entering northern industry, it had usually been against the opposition of a union. Fifth, unions had failed to do anything about the major grievance of black meat packing employees—lack of job advancement. Negroes entered the industry in the most undesirable jobs, as had the European ethnic groups which preceded them. But where the Europeans had moved on to better jobs, Negroes, with some exceptions during the labor shortages of World War I, had not.[53] Had unions strongly espoused the cause of job advancement, they would undoubtedly have obtained more support from black workers. Sixth, Negroes in Chicago and, no doubt, in other cities, increasingly encountered racially restrictive practices after the beginning of the rapid migration to the North. The meat packing strike of 1921-22 was seen as a race issue by many blacks, one which offered a means of retaliation against discrimination by whites.

All of these explanations have validity. Another, more general, interpretation can also be offered. It may be argued that the Negro's most fundamental mistrust of meat packing unions arose from an obvious prejudice on the part of whites toward

---

[51] *Ibid.*, pp. 59-60.

[52] *Ibid.*, p. 60.

[53] *Ibid.*, pp. xix-xx, 61-62; Chicago Commission on Race Relations, *op. cit.*, pp. 364, 390; Spero and Harris, *op. cit.*, p. 268.

him, a prejudice evidenced in a variety of interpersonal and community relations, but particularly in housing segregation. Kerr and Siegel have advanced the hypothesis that union militancy frequently occurs when the workers of an industry live together but are not socially and politically integrated into the larger community; physically demanding job tasks are seen to add to this tendency. In such circumstances, the occupational composition of the community becomes overriding and a consensus on grievances and their remedies often develops.[54]

This hypothesis applies well to the white workers in the Chicago meat packing industry during the first quarter of this century. Almost all lived in an area which came to be called "back-of-the-yards." Each successive group of European immigrants who came into the industry moved into residences in that area—but Negroes did not. They were forced to live in residential areas more than a mile to the east of the yards.[55]

> The southern Negroes who flocked to Chicago to work in the packinghouses and steel mills during the wartime boom found an already well developed black enclave on the South Side. Negroes were systemmatically excluded from white sections of the city, drastically limited in their choice of jobs, and barred from many places of public accommodation.[56]

Negroes could not become part of the homogeneous back-of-the-yards community where the specter of meat packing employment hung over every waking hour of almost all residents. This fact had direct effects upon race relations among stockyard employees. Some of the racial antagonism which developed in Chicago during World War I was over complaints by white clerical workers, who rode the elevated transit lines, that Negro stockyard laborers, who also rode the lines, were dirty and foul smelling.[57] Negro laborers were forced to use the transit system

---

[54] Clark Kerr and Abraham Siegel, "The Interindustry Propensity to Strike—An International Comparison," in A. Kornhauser, R. Dubin and A. Ross (eds.), *Industrial Conflict* (New York: McGraw-Hill, 1954), pp. 189-212.

[55] See Sophonisba P. Breckinridge and Edith Abbott, "Housing Conditions in Chicago, III: Back of the Yards," *American Journal of Sociology*, Vol. 16 (January 1911), pp. 433-468.

[56] Spear, *op. cit.*, p. ix.

[57] Chicago Commission on Race Relations, *op. cit.*, p. 620.

to get to work from their residences well to the east of the yards, while white laborers could walk from their homes immediately to the west of the yards.[58]

Although employees of meat packing firms were just a small fraction of all residents of the black ghetto, they were no doubt much better integrated into the general Negro community than were white workers into the larger white community. It is not surprising that in these circumstances black workers failed to develop the emotional fervor which would have been necessary to support precarious unions and quixotic strikes in one of the few manufacturing industries which had employed them in large numbers. This explanation has most relevance to the Chicago meat industry, but it also applies fairly well to other centers of the industry, particularly East St. Louis, Kansas City, and Omaha, where black workers were cut off residentially from their white counterparts.

When Negro packinghouse workers finally did support unions, in the 1930's and 1940's, the circumstances had changed considerably. Union activity had become legally protected under the National Labor Relations Act and workers in large-scale manufacturing were rapidly organizing. The fervent, all consuming commitment which had been prerequisite to support of unions in the jungle of industrial relations that had prevailed earlier was no longer necessary.

RIOTS

The story of Negro employment gains during World War I should not be concluded without consideration of the race riots which occurred in East St. Louis, Chicago, and Omaha. These acts of violence took place in all three cities as rapid immigration of Negroes to take jobs created by the wartime boom was occurring. In all three cities, meat packing was a major employer of the migrating blacks.

---

[58] Neither the back-of-the-yards area nor the south side "Black Belt" were pleasant places to live. The back-of-the-yards was bordered on the east by the stockyards, on the west by city dumps, on the north by "Bubbly Creek"—used for the disposal of packing plant refuse—and on the south by railroad tracks. The south side black areas were not confined by such unpleasant borders; still, only 26 percent of the houses in the Negro areas were in "good" condition compared with 54 percent in the stockyards area. Also, rents in the black area were higher, the median for a four-room apartment being $12.00 a week compared to just over $8.00 in the back-of-the-yards. (Alzada P. Comstock, "Chicago Housing Conditions VI: The Problem of the Negro," *American Journal of Sociology*, Vol. 18 (September 1912), pp. 252-255.)

East St. Louis

East St. Louis in 1917 was a heavily industrialized, notoriously misgoverned city of 60,000 persons. Meat packing was the major industry; Armour, Swift, and Morris were major employers of the city's workers. The interest of these packing firms in their workers, however, stopped at the plant gates. Support for community welfare in East St. Louis was not forthcoming from the meat industry. On the contrary, the packing firms incorporated their own municipality in order to obtain low property tax assessments.[59]

Racial tensions in East St. Louis were built up, as previously described, by increases in the employment of Negroes immediately preceding World War I and by the collapse of labor unions. The latter was a result of vigorous antiunion efforts by meat packing employers in 1916 and 1917 and by the Aluminum Ore Company in 1917. Exaggeration by union leaders and other members of the community of employer intentions to bring in more Negro workers further heightened tensions. On May 23, 1919, the following letter was distributed:[60]

> To the Delegates to the Central Trades and Labor Union
>
> Greetings: The immigration of the southern Negro into our city for the past eight months has reached the point where drastic action must be taken if we intend to work and live peaceably in this community.
>
> Since this influx of undersirable Negroes has started, no less than 10,000 have come into this locality.
>
> These men are being used to the detriment of our white citizens by some of the capitalists and a few of the real estate owners.
>
> On next Monday evening the entire body of delegates to the Central Trades and Labor Union will call upon the mayor and city council and demand that they take some action to retard this growing menace and also devise a way to get rid of a certain portion of those who are already here.

---

[59] Rudwick, *op. cit.*, pp. 148-156, 193-194.

[60] U.S. Bureau of Labor, *Negro Migration in 1916-17*, *op. cit.*, p. 131.

This is not a protest against the Negro who has been a long resident of East St. Louis and is a law-abiding citizen.

We earnestly request that you be in attendance on next Monday evening at 8 o'clock, at 137 Collinsville Avenue, where we will meet and then go to the city hall.

This is more important than any local meeting, so be sure you are there.

Fraternally,

Central Trades and Labor Union

Control of the meeting which this letter announced soon passed out of the hands of the union leaders, and emotional speeches were made exhorting the persons in attendance to take their own action should the authorities not act. Violence broke out almost immediately following the conclusion of the meeting, ignited by the shooting of a white woman by a Negro robber. The initial violence subsided without any deaths, but resumed again on July 1. Within two days, nine whites and at least thirty-nine blacks had been killed. Some estimates of the Negro deaths, including that of the East St. Louis Police Department, were much higher. In this small city of economically insecure, working class people, emotional fervor against the 10,000 Negro residents quickly encompassed much of the white population and brought disastrous results.[61]

Chicago

In Chicago there had also been a buildup of racial tensions following the greatly increased employment of black workers in meat packing and in other industries; but the riot which occurred in that city in the summer of 1919 was not as directly associated with labor disputes and Negro-white competition over jobs as was the case in East St. Louis. Nevertheless, the increase in racial hostilities over housing and use of public facilities which preceded the violence in Chicago would not have taken place in the absence of the great job-oriented migration of Negroes to that city. Meat packing, as the largest employing industry in the city, was of great importance to that migration.

The Chicago riot began on Sunday, July 27, 1919, with the drowning of a black boy after he had been stoned by whites

---

[61] Rudwick, *op. cit.*, pp. 50-52.

for crossing over an imaginary color line at a public beach. In the week which followed, 23 Negroes and 15 whites died. Even though race relations in the Union Stock Yards were probably better than in most other places of employment in the city, the stockyards were closely connected with the violence which occurred.[62]

Youthful white gangs waited to attack Negroes as they returned home from their packing plant jobs on the Monday following the outbreak of the riot. Forty-one percent of those injured in the violence received their injuries in the stockyards district. One Negro and two white men were killed either as they went to or returned from their jobs in the yards. Another Negro was killed inside the yards, after being attacked near the office of a superintendent of Swift and Company. On August 2, almost a week after the start of violence, incendiary fires, most likely set by persons attempting to stir up retaliation against Negroes, destroyed 49 houses in a Lithuanian neighborhood near the stockyards.[63]

Most Negro workers stayed away from the stockyards during the ten days following the outbreak of violence. When they returned, under the protection of police and soldiers arranged by the packers, the Stock Yards Labor Council called a strike to protest the presence of the military. This abortive strike, though its goal was recognition of the unions by the packers, further increased the hostility between white and black workers.[64]

Omaha

Less than two months after the Chicago riot, racial violence broke out in Omaha. This city had been a major meat industry center since the late 1880's when Armour, Cudahy, and Swift had been given land and other subsidies to induce them to locate large facilities in South Omaha. Black workers first came into Omaha meat packing as strikebreakers in 1895. During World War I, there was rapid migration of Negroes to the city and to jobs in the packing plants. As in other meat industry cities,

---

[62] Chicago Commission on Race Relations, *op. cit.*, pp. 1-50; Spear, *op. cit.*, p. 216.

[63] Chicago Commission on Race Relations, *op. cit.*, pp. 9, 15, 20-21, 400; Herbst, *op. cit.*, pp. 45, 50-51; Spear, *op. cit.*, p. 216.

[64] Brody, *op. cit.*, p. 88.

organized labor—frustrated by the failure of a meat packing strike in the summer of 1919—fanned rumors which exaggerated the number of black workers who were arriving in the city.[65]

During the spring and summer of 1919, a number of assaults on white women and other crimes were alleged to have been committed by Negroes. Whether there were factual bases for these charges, they were believed by many whites, in part because some of the Omaha newspapers printed them as facts. In late September, a white woman who had been walking with a partially crippled male companion was assaulted, and a forty-year-old Negro packinghouse worker was charged with the crime. The next evening, a large mob set fire to the county courthouse which contained the jail where the prisoner was being held. After retreating to the roof of the building with 100 prisoners, the sheriff turned the alleged Negro rapist over to the crowd. The frenzied mob hung its victim from a telephone pole, riddled the body with bullets, and, finally, stripped and burned it on one of the city's main streets. The mayor was badly injured when he attempted to stop the rioters and a number of Negroes were attacked and injured before the state militia was called.[66]

Concluding Comments on Riots

These three riots aptly illustrate a major inadequacy of America's economic system as it operated during the first part of this century. Prosperous business conditions during World War I and the cessation of immigration created incentives for employers to develop new supplies of labor. Employers turned to the Negro for this purpose. Meat packing firms, along with others, sent out the call and black workers from the South responded to the opportunities. The packers benefitted directly from this process of re-allocating labor, but they recognized no responsibility to the larger community for the social problems which arose from the re-allocation. In the folklore of the times, everything would have been all right if only whites, as workers and

---

[65] Alfred R. Sorenson, *The Story of Omaha*, Third Edition (Omaha: National Printing Company, 1923), pp. 604-606; Arthur V. Age, "The Omaha Riot of 1919," Master's Thesis, Dept. of History, Creighton University, 1964, pp. 31-32.

[66] Age, *loc. cit.*; Sorenson, *op. cit.*, pp. 645-647.

citizens, had yielded to the discipline of the system. But in the circumstances which have been described, it was pure fantasy to expect acquiescence from whites, many of whom were recent immigrants to the country who regarded themselves as living in very undesirable economic and social circumstances. Instead, white workers combined in their place of work to try to obtain job security and improve their economic livelihood, and in their community responded to the increasing numbers of Negroes by attempting to contain them behind a wall of discrimination. The latter was partially motivated by the threat which Negroes constituted to the work place organizations—the unions.

One can look at the history of that period and easily find fault with all participants; the packers for their seeming indifference to anything except their own profits; Negroes for their willingness to break strikes of lowly paid workers; and white unionists and citizens for their failure fully to embrace Negro workers within their unions, and for their social discrimination. But in the socioeconomic setting of the time, how could any of the participants have behaved differently? All were acting in what they perceived to be their self-interest. The packers had by far the greatest ability to alter the course of events which finally led to tragedy. But they never used that power; radically innovative social behavior was not one of the characteristics of meat packing employers. Persons of influence in the nation and citizens generally, through their government, could have become concerned with social problems created by the war production effort, but, instead, all immediate attention was devoted to the war itself and, later, to the return to "normalcy."

CHAPTER IV

From World War I to 1960: Changing Racial Employment Patterns

The turbulence which was associated with the Negro in the meat industry through the World War I era did not continue after 1921. Unions were absent from the industry during the twenties and most of the thirties; when they reappeared on the scene, in the late 1930's, there were fewer black workers and the racial conflict which had previously occurred between black and white workers was not repeated. World War II saw Negroes return to the industry in large numbers and without violence; then came the culmination of long-run changes in the industry during the 1950's when many black (and white) workers lost meat packing jobs in big cities and a large number of Negro women obtained jobs in the low-wage poultry sector of the industry. This chapter describes these events and concludes with an analysis of the union role in race relations in this era.

EMPLOYMENT DECLINES IN PROSPERITY AND DEPRESSION

The technology of meat slaughtering and butchering, as stated previously, was well advanced early in the history of the industry. The specialization of labor was highly developed before the turn of the century around overhead conveyors which were used to transport livestock carcasses through the various butchering stages. (The conveyors, purportedly, were the inspiration for Henry Ford's automobile assembly lines.)

These techniques, however, did not enable the meat industry to raise its productivity—lower its ratio of workers to units of output—between 1890 and 1920. Rather, during the last decade of the nineteenth century the ratio of production employees (manual workers through the working foreman level) to units of output rose by an average annual rate of 3.9 percent.[67] There was no change in unit-worker requirements between 1900 and 1910, and, in the decade of World War I, workers per unit of

---

[67] Solomon Fabricant, *Employment in Manufacturing, 1899-1939* (New York: National Bureau of Economic Research, 1942), p. 65.

product again rose—this time at an annual rate of 3.5 percent.[68] The major forces which brought about the declining labor productivity were increases in the processed meat proportion of total output (more industry labor went into the processed meats than into the fresh cuts), inefficient utilization of labor in periods of high output, especially the war period, and declines in weekly hours of work.

The Twenties

In the 1920's, however, meat packing, as well as the rest of American industry, obtained large gains in labor productivity. The chief technical innovations of the period in the meat industry were the development and application of electric motors and power equipment to a variety of operations, including depilation and butchering. According to the general superintendent of Armour and Company, the use of mechanical and electrical power, "due to applications of labor saving equipment," increased by approximately 600 percent between 1915 and 1930.[69] These and other technical changes reduced unit-worker requirements at the rate of 3.4 percent a year during the 1920's.[70] Although this was still below the performance of most manufacturing industries, it represented a substantial improvement over the previous 30 years in the history of the meat industry.

Output between 1920 and 1930 grew by almost 10 percent, but these gains were not nearly enough to offset the increases which took place in labor productivity. Therefore, employment in the meat industry declined sharply during the 1920's. *The Census of Manufactures* discloses that production worker employment fell from 160,900 in 1919 to 122,500 in 1929, a decline of almost one-fourth (Appendix Table A-3). The employment peak of 1919 was not attained again until World War II.

Changes in Negro employment over this period can be obtained from the decennial census of population, as shown in

---

[68] The comparative performance of the meat industry with respect to gains in labor productivity was also very poor; the industry ranked forty-sixth out of fifty-one manufacturing industries over the period 1899-1937. During this period, unit worker requirements actually increased by 0.3 percent a year, compared to a decline for all manufacturing of 1.8 percent a year. (Fabricant, *op. cit.*, p. 45.)

[69] Myrick D. Harding, "Mechanical Progress in Meat Packing," *Journal of the Western Society of Engineers*, Vol. 42, No. 1 (1937), p. 28.

[70] Fabricant, *op. cit.*, p. 65.

Table 10, p. 28. The number of black workers in the meat industry fell from an estimated 30,000 in 1920 to a little over 20,000 in 1930, while the total number of employed workers declined less rapidly. The change in the Negro percentage of employment was from 15.2 to 11.8. The number of low-skilled Negro workers in the industry fell during the decade from 28,000 to less than 19,000, or from 21.4 to 17.7 percent. (Table 12.) Thus, in this period of rapid gains in labor productivity, Negro employment declined more sharply than did employment of whites.

TABLE 12. *Meat Industry*
Low-skilled Employment, Selected Locations, 1920 and 1930

Location	Total Employment		Negro Employment		Percent Negro	
	1920	1930	1920	1930	1920	1930
Six Leading Centers						
Chicago[a]	32,920	19,720	8,600	6,150	26.1	31.2
Kansas City, Kan.	6,830	3,870	2,210	1,260	32.4	32.6
Kansas City, Mo.	3,670	1,360	1,740[b]	630[b]	47.4	46.3
Omaha	7,200	4,210	1,470	920	20.4	21.9
St. Louis	3,780	2,120[b]	2,290[b]	780[b]	60.6	36.8
Indianapolis	2,920	2,160	1,220[c]	780[c]	41.8	36.1
Six City Total	57,320	33,440	17,530	10,520	30.6	31.5
Rest of U.S.[a]	75,070	71,500	10,800	8,070	14.4	11.3
U.S. Total[a]	132,390	104,940	28,330	18,590	21.4	17.7
Six City Percentage of U.S. Employment	43.3	31.9	61.9	56.6		

Source: *U.S. Census of Population: 1920*, Vol. IV; *1930*, Vol. V.
Note: Table includes operative and laborer occupational classifications.
[a] Includes "stockyard" laborers (see Appendix Table A-1).
[b] Males only; female figures not available.
[c] Does not include female laborers.

The most important contributor to the relative decline of Negro employment was the sharp decline in meat packing which took place in the urban centers of the industry. It was in these cities that black workers had obtained their greatest representation during the war; when the war-swollen employment in Chicago, Kansas City, and other centers of the meat industry was sharply reduced in the early 1920's, the effect on Negro employment in the entire industry was substantial. Table 12 shows that between 1920 and 1930 the number of low-skilled jobs in the meat industry declined by 27,450 and that almost 24,000 of these job losses occurred in six large urban centers. The share of industry employment held by these cities fell from 43.3 percent in 1920 to 31.9 percent 10 years later (Table 12).

Negro representation in the six industry centers—defined as the Negro *percentage* of employment—remained stable despite the declines in total employment which took place in these locations. In Greater Kansas City, Omaha, and Indianapolis, the Negro percentage of low-skilled employment was about the same at the end of the decade as at the beginning. The Negro percentage in St. Louis declined from the very high level at which it stood in 1920, but this was more than offset by an increase in the Negro fraction of employment in Chicago. Thus, even though their share of industry employment fell sharply, the six urban centers experienced only a small decline in their share of the industry's Negro employment—from 61.9 to 56.6 percent (Table 12).

The decline in importance of the older meat packing centers which occurred in the 1920's was associated with shifts in the location of meat industry employment. The locational changes can be shown most clearly with *Census of Manufactures* data because they are available for the peak employment year of 1919. In that year, the four leading meat packing states employed 56.2 percent of all production workers; by 1929 they employed only 41.2 percent (Table 13). Iowa and Minnesota increased their share of industry employment, as did New York, Indiana, and Ohio, and the South and West regions. Negro employment was relatively small in all of these industry locations.

The decentralization of the meat industry away from metropolitan centers—a movement which is still going on—will be more fully discussed below. The impact of this movement on Negro employment in the industry is clear, however, even from this brief discussion: Negro employment was reduced below what it would have been in the absence of decentralization. This occurred because the general direction of changes in industry location was away from metropolitan centers which contained many black people to small cities and towns which contained few or none.

TABLE 13. *Meat Industry*
Production Workers, Selected States and by Region
1919 and 1929

	Production Workers[a]		Percent of U. S. Total	
Four Leading States	1919	1929	1919	1929
Illinois	54.2	29.6	33.7	24.2
Kansas	17.8	9.1	11.1	7.4
Nebraska	10.1	6.1	6.3	5.0
Missouri	8.3	5.6	5.1	4.6
Total	90.4	50.4	56.2	41.2
Next Five Leading States				
Iowa	7.1	8.7	4.4	7.1
New York	6.6	7.3	4.1	6.0
Indiana	5.7	5.0	3.5	4.1
Ohio	5.3	5.8	3.3	4.7
Minnesota	5.2	6.9	3.2	5.6
Total	29.9	33.7	18.5	27.5
Regions				
Northeast	19.9	18.6	12.4	15.2
East North Central	70.1	45.6	43.5	37.2
West North Central	50.7	38.4	31.5	31.4
South	12.1	11.6	7.5	9.4
West	8.1	8.3	5.1	6.8
Total U. S.	160.9	122.5	100.0	100.0

Source: *U. S. Census of Manufactures*, 1919 and 1929; U. S. Bureau of the Census, *Location of Manufactures 1899-1929* (Washington: Government Printing Office, 1933).

Note: For regional definitions, see Table 4, p. 9.

[a] Manual workers through the foreman level.

A second contributor to Negro employment losses of the decade was a reduction in the Negro percentage of employment in industry locations outside of the metropolitan centers. Industry employment outside of the six cities previously mentioned fell by more than 3,500 during the twenties, and Negro employment in these locations declined by over 2,700 (Table 12). This experience stands in contrast to that of black workers in the six industry centers, where, in spite of large losses of total employment, the Negro percentage of employment was maintained.

Finally, a change in the skill requirements of the industry may have contributed to the relative decline of Negro employment. There was a decrease of approximately 13,500 unskilled (laborer) jobs in the meat industry during the 1920's, while the number of semiskilled (operative) positions increased by 3,000. Since, traditionally, black workers had been better represented in unskilled than semiskilled jobs, the relative decrease in unskilled work had a greater employment impact on blacks than on whites. The meat industry in the 1920's eliminated many of the unskilled employees who had been hired to meet wartime production schedules; Negroes were heavily represented in this group.

The Thirties

Employment in manufacturing declined sharply during the depression of the 1930's, and the meat industry shared in the employment losses which took place in the early part of the decade. By 1931, the number of production workers in the industry had fallen to 107,000 from 123,000 in 1929. Thereafter, employment increased slowly until 1937 and then fell back, in 1939, to a level which was just below that of ten years earlier.

The decennial population censuses show that between 1930 and 1940 the number of Negroes employed in the meat industry fell from 20,400, or 11.8 percent of the work force, to 16,200, or 7.7 percent (Table 10, p. 28). Thus, in the twenty years which followed the end of World War I, Negro employment in the industry declined by approximately one-half, both in absolute numbers and as a proportion of all workers.

Although there is almost no direct evidence on the subject, it is not difficult to explain the decline in Negro employment which took place during the 1930's. The high unemployment of the depression years increased the number of white workers who were willing to take jobs in the packinghouses. Whites who lost their jobs in construction, durable goods manufacturing, and other hard-hit industries were forced to look for jobs which they previously would not have taken. Jobs were available in the meat industry because of the high worker turnover and seasonal characteristics of the industry. The increased availability of white workers led to an increase in their proportion of total employment over the decade, at the expense of a reduced proportion for black workers.

In his history of unionism in meat packing, a union official who was active in the organizing campaigns of the thirties stated that, "during the depression when jobs were scarce, Swift had started to weed out Negroes." [71] The statement suggests that the decline in Negro employment which occurred between 1930 and 1940 may have been the deliberate outcome of policies followed by one or more leading firms in the industry. A decline in Negro employment, however, could have occurred in the absence of any such policy. Employment during the depression fell most sharply in the cyclical industries such as durable goods manufacturing and construction, and these industries employed smaller proportions of Negroes than did meat packing. No doubt the proportion of whites in the pool of labor which was available to the meat industry rose during the depression, along with an increase in the average qualifications of white applicants—in the 1950's a number of the ablest foremen at Swift's Chicago facilities had first been employed by the company in the 1930's.[72] Of course, Negro unemployment also increased in the depression, but despair over the probabilities of getting a job probably kept down the number of Negroes seeking employment in the industry.[73]

The job losses suffered by black workers, to an even greater extent than in the previous decade, occurred in the six cities of Chicago, Kansas City, Kansas, Kansas City, Missouri, St. Louis, Indianapolis, and Omaha. Now, however, the losses were not

---

[71] Arthur Kampfert, "History of Meat Packing, Slaughtering and Unionism," unpublished manuscript, files of the United Packinghouse Workers of America, Chicago, 1949, Part II, pp. 6-8.

[72] Theodore V. Purcell, *The Worker Speaks His Mind* (Cambridge: Harvard University Press, 1953), p. 33.

[73] See Herbst, *op. cit.*, p. 106 for evidence that in one medium-sized meat packing plant in Chicago, the Negro proportion of job applicants varied inversely with the general level of employment.

attributable so much to declining employment in these centers as they were the result of reduced Negro shares of employment. Table 14, which presents the relevant information for the four cities for which precise comparisons between 1930 and 1940 can be made, shows that the Negro percentages of low-skilled meat industry employment declined sharply in all four locations. Low-skilled employment in these four cities declined by about 1,000 during the decade; however, the number of black workers fell by approximately 3,200. In addition, the author's estimates from census data indicate that Negro meat packing employment in Kansas City, Kansas, and Omaha (cities for which precise comparisons of 1940 with 1930 cannot be made) fell by approximately 800 and 300, respectively, during the thirties. Thus, these six urban centers of the industry reduced their employment of Negroes by 4,300, a figure approximately equal to the total number of jobs lost by Negroes in the entire industry.

TABLE 14. *Meat Industry*
Low-Skilled Employment in Four Cities, 1930 and 1940

	Total Employment		Negro Employment		Percent Negro	
	1930	1940	1930	1940	1930	1940
Chicago	19,720[a]	18,860	6,150[a]	3,700	31.2	19.6
Kansas City, Mo.	1,360[b]	1,192	630[b]	420	46.3	35.2
St. Louis	2,120	2,430	780	620	36.8	25.5
Indianapolis	2,160[c]	1,720	780[c]	390	36.1	22.7
Total	25,360	24,202	8,340	5,130	32.9	21.2

Source: *U.S. Census of Population: 1930*, Vol. V; *1940*, Vol. III.

[a] Includes stockyard laborers (see Appendix Table A-1).

[b] Males only; female figures not available.

[c] Does not include female laborers.

Negro employment in the rest of the industry—outside of the six metropolitan centers—remained constant during the decade. The Negro percentage of employment did fall, however, as total (white) employment increased in this part of the industry.

It is likely that Negro employment in the meat industry during the depression held up better in the South than elsewhere. A 1937 survey by the Bureau of Labor Statistics covering about one-half of meat packing employment disclosed that one-fourth of all production workers in the South were black, while the comparable fraction for the North was just one-tenth.[74] Only about 10 percent of the industry was located in the South at that time, however.

Changes in the location of the meat industry continued to occur in the thirties. The share of employment held by the states of Illinois, Kansas, Missouri, and Nebraska—the four leading states in the industry at the end of World War I—declined from 41.2 to 33.4 percent over the decade. (See Appendix Table A-3.) Iowa and Minnesota continued to increase in relative importance, as did the West and, especially, the South.

These locational shifts, with the exception of movement to the South, had an adverse effect on Negro employment because so few black workers were available in the West North Central and West. Still, by far the most important influence on Negro employment in the meat industry during the 1930's was the reduction which occurred in the percentage of Negro employment in industry locations where black workers had long been employed in large numbers, as white workers replaced many of the black workers in these locations.

THE WORLD WAR II IMPACT

Employment in the meat industry grew rapidly during World War II from the depression level of 1939. Bureau of Labor Statistics data show that total employment in the industry increased from 201,000 in 1939 to 267,000 in 1942.[75] Negro employment between the decennial census years of 1940 and 1950 rose from 16,152 to 39,130 (Table 15). The Negro share of employment almost doubled in the decade, increasing from 7.7 percent in 1940 to 14.3 percent ten years later. No doubt, most of the job gains of black workers occurred during the first half of the decade, the war period.

As in 1916-18, the major force behind the increase in Negro employment during the 1940's was the shortage of labor caused by the war. The war sharply reversed the loose labor markets of the Great Depression which had brought about a decline in the use of Negroes in meat packing. Between 1939 and 1942,

---

[74] "Earnings and Hours in the Meat Packing Industry, December 1937," *Monthly Labor Review*, Vol. 39 (October 1939), p. 953.

[75] U.S. Bureau of Labor Statistics, *Employment and Earnings for the United States, 1909-62*, Bulletin No. 1312-1, 1963, p. 316.

the labor requirements of the meat industry rose in response to production for the war effort, while at the same time, movement of men into the armed forces and to more desirable industries drained the usual labor supplies. Meat packing employers, therefore, turned to groups which previously had not been fully utilized—women and Negroes.

Women had comprised 15 percent of the work force in the meat industry in 1940; by 1950 they made up 21 percent. (See Appendix Table A-1.) Negro women, especially, gained from the increased use of the fairer sex. Beginning in the 1920's and continuing until World War II, the major meat packing firms hired very few Negro women; thus, only 1,200 were employed in 1940 compared to over 2,000 in 1920. This seemingly discriminatory practice was dropped under the pressure of wartime labor markets and, by 1950, 6,300 Negro women held jobs in the meat industry, though many of these were in low-wage poultry processing. Negro women as a percentage of all female employees rose from 2.5 to 11.3 in this decade (Appendix Table A-1).

Also, as in 1916-18, the urban meat packing centers of the North accounted for most of the increases in black employment. Jobs held by Negroes rose by nearly 23,000 between 1940 and 1950 (Table 15), and almost 10,000 of these jobs were obtained in four northern industry centers—Chicago, Greater Kansas City, St. Louis, and Omaha.[76] In Chicago alone, employment of Negroes increased by over 6,000, and Negroes became a majority of the work force in many plants.[77] Now, however, in contrast to the experience of World War I, many Negroes—about 8,000 —obtained jobs in the southern meat industry by 1950 (Table 15). In part, this was a result of the growing southern proportion of industry employment, but, in addition, Negroes increased their share of meat industry employment in the South itself. The Negro percentage of meat products workers in the South rose from 14.6 in 1940 to 22.8 in 1950. One-third of all black workers employed in the meat industry in 1950 were in the South, 43.4 percent were in the four largest urban centers of the industry and 19.5 percent were in other locations of the North (Table 16).

---

[76] This figure is a rough estimate from *U. S. Census of Population, 1940* and *1950;* the census data do not allow precise comparison of 1940 and 1950 for Greater Kansas City and Omaha.

[77] Purcell, *Worker Speaks, op. cit.,* p. 30.

TABLE 15. Meat Industry
Total and Negro Employment by Region
1940-1960

Region	All Employees			Negro			Percent Negro		
	1940	1950	1960	1940	1950	1960	1940	1950	1960
Northeast	33,339	35,774	43,146	1,063	2,480	4,238	3.2	6.9	9.8
North Central	123,115	156,105	153,486	9,622	22,132	16,014	7.8	14.2	10.4
South	36,149	57,679	89,656	5,278	13,179	21,970	14.6	22.8	24.5
West	17,522	24,308	31,723	189	1,339	1,658	1.1	5.5	5.2
Total U. S.	210,123	273,866	318,011	16,152	39,130	43,880	7.7	14.3	13.8

Source: *U. S. Census of Population:*

1940, Vol. III, *The Labor Force*, Part 1, Table 77.
1950, Vol. II, *Characteristics of the Population*, Part 1, Table 161.
1960, PC (1), 1D, *U. S. Summary*, Table 260.

Note: For regional definitions, see Table 4, p. 9.

TABLE 16. *Meat Industry*
Percentage Distribution of Total and Negro Employment
by Region
1940-1960

Region	Total			Negro		
	1940	1950	1960	1940	1950	1960
Northeast	15.9	13.1	13.6	6.6	6.3	9.6
North Central	58.6	57.0	48.2	59.5	56.6	36.5
South	17.2	21.1	28.2	32.7	33.7	50.1
West	8.3	8.8	10.0	1.2	3.4	3.8
	100.0	100.0	100.0	100.0	100.0	100.0
Four Northern Centers[a]	n.a.	23.1	13.1	n.a.	43.4	23.3

Source: Computed from Table 15.

Note: For regional definitions, see Table 4, p. 9.

[a] The Chicago, Kansas City, Omaha, and St. Louis metropolitan areas.

INDUSTRY CHANGES, *1947-1960*

After World War II, Negro employment in the meat industry was influenced by several far-reaching changes in the industry. The major changes were in employment, plant location, and firm concentration. Before describing these changes it should be noted that in 1940 the Bureau of the Census began to refer to the activity under discussion as the "meat products" industry. The adoption of this term reflected the fact that meat processing as well as poultry dressing and processing had become significant components of meat manufacturing. Meat packing, however, continued to be the largest part of the meat industry, in terms of employment, sales, or any other measure.

Falling Employment

Employment in meat products advanced after World War II to a peak of approximately 324,000 in 1956. It then declined slowly to a level of 300,000 in 1962-63. There has been a modest recovery within the last few years, particularly in 1967 when employment rose to 305,000. (See Table 5, p. 11.) However, in the long period of uninterrupted economic prosperity which the

United States has enjoyed since 1961, increases in employment
have been much smaller in the meat industry than in most other
manufacturing sectors.[78]

Since output of meat products has grown throughout the postwar period—the dressed meat output of the meat packing sector
rose from 20 billion pounds in 1947 to 31 billion pounds in
1966—the declines in employment have been a result of increases in output per worker. These were relatively slow between 1947 and 1956, but, apparently, have picked up markedly
since then. According to the U. S. Bureau of Labor Statistics,
employment in meat packing declined by 11 percent between
1947 and 1962, while the amount of meat produced rose by 24
percent.[79] These figures imply that output per worker rose at
an average annual rate of 2.25 percent over the period. It is
known that output per worker increased by something less than
2 percent between 1947 and 1956, so very sizeable gains in labor
productivity must have occurred after the latter date.[80]

The recent improvements in productivity are associated with
marked technological changes in the manufacture of meat products, particularly in the meat packing sector of the industry.
Among the large firms, Armour, in the early 1950's, began a
program of modernization which drastically reduced its labor
requirements.[81] Recently, new firms have been entering the industry, employing efficient plant layouts and automated production techniques which require relatively few employees. Iowa
Beef Packing is the outstanding example of this development.
Organized in 1960, this firm is now the sixth largest in the industry, yet it employed only 2,200 workers in 1968, compared

---

[78] Between 1961 and 1967, employment increased by 3 percent in the meat
products industry and by 18 percent in all of manufacturing. These data are
computed from U.S. Bureau of Labor Statistics, *Employment and Earnings
in the United States, 1909-68*, Bulletin No. 1312-6, 1968, pp. 48, 460.

[79] U.S. Bureau of Labor Statistics, *Industry Wage Survey, Meat Products*,
Bulletin No. 1415, 1964, p. 2.

[80] For labor productivity figures covering various periods between 1947 and
1958, see John Kendrick, *Productivity Trends in the United States* (Princeton:
Princeton University Press, 1961), p. 483; Herrell DeGraff, *Beef Production
and Distribution* (Oklahoma City: University of Oklahoma Press, 1960),
pp. 172-173; and Milton Derber, "Economic Trends in the Meat Packing
Industry with Particular Reference to Employment Prospects as of 1975,"
unpublished manuscript, 1961, courtesy Professor Derber.

[81] George P. Shultz and Arnold R. Weber, *Strategies for the Displaced
Worker* (New York: Harper & Row, 1966), p. vii.

to the 8,292 employed by Hormel which had only slightly larger sales. (See Table 3, p. 6.) Iowa Beef's sales per worker in 1968 were among the largest of any manufacturing firm in the country.[82] Laborsaving changes in technology will apparently continue in the foreseeable future even though some firms are planning to do much of the meat processing which is now done in retail stores. In the fall of 1968, Swift announced a large modernization program which will close some of its oldest and largest facilities, open some new ones, and reduce the firm's employment by perhaps as many as 14,000 persons.[83]

The three divisions of the meat products industry have shown different employment trends since 1947. (See Table 5, p. 11.) In the oldest and largest division, meat packing, employment has fallen by almost 20 percent (through 1967), and in the meat processing division, it has risen slightly. Employment in the poultry division, however, has increased more than threefold as Americans increased their consumption of ready-to-cook chicken broilers and other fowl. Most of this change occurred during the 1950's. Meat packing, which in pre-World War II days employed upwards of 80 percent of all meat industry employees, now has less than 50 percent while poultry dressing and processing has increased its share from under one-tenth in 1947 to more than one-quarter in 1967.

Contrary to the trends in some other industries, the white collar fraction (as measured by nonproduction workers) of meat industry employment has not increased since 1947, but has remained at about one-fifth for the industry as a whole. In meat packing the white collar fraction has increased slightly, but this has been offset by the growth of the poultry division where relatively few white collar workers are employed.

Decentralization

Decentralization of meat products manufacturing, a trend confined principally to meat packing, has occurred at least since the turn of the century when more than one-third of all industry employees were concentrated in Chicago and a sizeable fraction were in the Kansas City area. (See Appendix Table A-5.)

---

[82] In part, the large sales per worker enjoyed by Iowa Beef Packers are attributable to the firm's specialization in livestock slaughtering and packing; it does not perform the more labor-intensive meat processing activities.

[83] *Wall Street Journal*, November 29, 1968; Meyers, *loc. cit.*

At that time almost all commercial livestock slaughtering was done at these and other major railroad terminals. With improvements in the refrigerated railroad car, cost advantages over the older method were obtained by slaughtering animals near cattle-raising areas and transporting dressed or processed meat to metropolitan markets. These cost advantages brought about the slow decline of the older packing centers, a trend which has not yet ended. The dispersal of meat packing plants was slowed by the great production demands on the industry in World War I, but it resumed again in the twenties, aided by improved highways and motor truck technology.[84] World War II again slowed the long-run change process, but the trend to decentralization has resumed with new vigor since 1947. Within the last twenty years, many of the older plants in the industry have been shut down and their output absorbed by newer facilities in less urbanized areas.[85]

Along with the other factors mentioned, lower wage rates in small cities may have hastened the movement of meat plants into the livestock producing areas of the West North Central region during the 1920's and early 1930's. Low wages have also made a minor contribution to the southern expansion of the industry in more recent years.

The principal locations which have lost employment through the decentralization process have been the northern urban centers, especially Chicago. Beginning in 1950 with the closing of some of Swift's plants, all major meat packing firms have shut down their Chicago facilities, with the exception of a few processing plants. Very little livestock slaughtering is now performed in Chicago. The vast Union Stock Yards presently serve chiefly as a terminal from which livestock is shipped to eastern cities. Other traditional meat packing centers have been similarly affected. For example, only Swift maintains a major facility in the Kansas City area, and the meat industry in East St. Louis has been reduced to processing operations. Since 1960, Cudahy and Armour have closed most of their Omaha facilities and Swift

---

[84] It has been estimated that the percent of livestock and livestock products shipped by rail declined from 75 percent in 1935 to 25 percent in 1958. See Richard J. Arnould, "Changing Patterns of Concentration in the Meat Packing Industry," Master's thesis, Iowa State University, 1965, p. 22.

[85] National Commission on Food Marketing, *loc. cit.;* U.S. Department of Agriculture, *Agricultural Markets in Change,* Economic Research Service, Agriculture Economic Report No. 95, 1966, pp. 285-295; Arnould, *loc. cit.,* pp. 53-72.

will follow suit in the fall of 1969. Smaller operators have taken over some of the plants which were closed by the major firms in all of these locations, but meat industry employment in all of them is well below early postwar levels.

The areas which have gained employment in meat products from the long-term dislocations are the West North Central region, the South, and the West. (The changes can be seen most clearly, for the dominant meat packing division, in Appendix Table A-3.) Since 1947 only the latter two regions have experienced employment gains (Table 17).

To the extent that there is a center of the meat industry at present, it is located in a strip of cornbelt land, approximately 200 miles wide, which runs from east to west through northern Iowa and southern Minnesota. The largest meat plants in the country are now located in this strip and in contiguous locations, surrounded by the major sources of livestock supply. Cities with major plants include Cedar Rapids, Fort Dodge, Marshalltown, Mason City, Ottumwa, Sioux City, and Waterloo, Iowa; and Austin, Albert Lea, and St. Paul, Minnesota. Adjoining the Iowa-Minnesota area on the west are the remaining facilities in Omaha and the large Morrell plant in Sioux Falls, South Dakota. Oscar Mayer operates one of the industry's largest plants only a short distance to the east, in Madison, Wisconsin. It is now accurate to call meat products manufacturing a small-city industry, and this will be an increasingly proper designation with the passage of time.

Looking at states, Iowa now leads the nation in meat products employment; Minnesota is second, while Illinois and Kansas have only a fraction of their former prominence in the industry (employment, 1919-1963, in the meat packing sector of the industry is given for these and other states in Appendix Table A-3).

Employment growth in the meat industry since the end of World War II has occurred principally in the South. Its share of industry employment rose from 17.7 percent in 1947 to 31.2 percent in 1963 (Table 17). Easily the most important factor in that expansion has been the rapid growth of poultry processing. Between 1947 and 1963, this activity accounted for over 31,000 of 35,000 new production-worker jobs in the southern meat industry. Innovative use of former cotton-growing areas and ample supplies of labor, including that of Negroes, have caused most of the expansion of the nation's poultry processing to take

TABLE 17. *Meat Industry*
Production Worker Employment by Standard Industrial
Classification and Region
1947 and 1963

| | Total Meat Products | | | |
| | Employment | | Percent of U.S. Total | |
	1947	1963	1947	1963
Northeast	29,600	30,100	13.5	12.6
East North Central	60,800	43,700	27.5	18.3
West North Central	70,500	65,500	31.9	27.5
South	39,100	74,500	17.7	31.2
West	20,700	24,800	9.4	10.4
Total	220,700	238,600	100.0	100.0
Meat Packing				
Northeast	18,200	11,800	10.8	8.5
East North Central	47,100	27,400	28.2	19.8
West North Central	59,300	52,800	35.5	38.2
South	26,700	31,700	16.0	22.9
West	15,800	14,700	9.5	10.6
Total	167,100	138,400	100.0	100.0
Meat Processing				
Northeast	10,500	12,500	30.5	34.4
East North Central	12,500	11,400	36.2	31.4
West North Central	2,900	2,500	8.4	6.9
South	5,900	5,200	17.1	14.3
West	2,700	4,700	7.8	13.0
Total	34,500	36,300	100.0	100.0
Poultry				
Northeast	950	5,700	4.9	8.9
East North Central	1,200	4,900	6.3	7.7
West North Central	8,300	10,100	43.2	15.8
South	6,500	37,700	33.9	59.1
West	2,250	5,400	11.7	8.5
Total	19,200	63,800	100.0	100.0

Source: *U. S. Census of Manufactures:*

       1947, Vol. I, *General Summary*, Table 6.
       1963, Vol. II, *Industry Statistics*, Part 1, Meat Products, Table 2.

place in the South. The South, at present, employs three-fifths of all workers in this industry sector, while producing about 85 percent of the country's chicken broilers. The four states of Georgia, Arkansas, North Carolina, and Alabama alone employ almost one-third of all poultry workers.[86]

In the meat packing side of the industry, most of the southern expansion occurred in the 1940's, though the relative importance of the South in meat packing continued to increase into the 1960's (Appendix Table A-3). The growth of meat packing in the South was largely a response to increasing production of cattle in Oklahoma and Texas. Low wage rates in the South were an additional attraction—in 1963 average hourly earnings of packinghouse workers in the Southwest were $1.86 an hour as compared to $3.08 an hour in the Midwest.[87] The North-South wage differential currently is greater for meat packing than for any other major industry, including locally oriented ones such as eating places and hotels.[88] Undoubtedly, this differential was a factor noticed by many southern entrepreneurs in their efforts to capture local and regional markets from national packing firms whose product prices reflect high labor and transportation costs. Most independent southern packers are small and operate nonunion establishments, characteristics which have helped them to maintain low wages. National packers have responded to the challenge of the southern independents by establishing plants of their own in that region, but the advantages which they have been able to obtain have been limited by the unwillingness of the packinghouse unions to permit the existence of a large North-South wage differential within their bargaining jurisdiction. Only a small part of national packer operations are located in the South at present. In spite of low wages in nonunion plants, future expansion of meat packing in the South will be restricted by the limitations of the region as a livestock-producing area.

To the extent that employment increases do take place in meat packing—although presently decreases are more probable—they seem likely to occur in the West. California has already become

---

[86] *U. S. Census of Manufactures, 1963;* U. S. Department of Agriculture, *op. cit.,* p. 359.

[87] U.S. Bureau of Labor Statistics, *Industry Wage Survey, op. cit.,* p. 12.

[88] H.M. Douty, "Wage Differentials: Forces and Counterforces," *Monthly Labor Review,* Vol. XC (March 1968), pp. 74-81.

the second leading state for the slaughtering of cattle.[89] Efficient, large-scale feed lot operations are becoming increasingly important in the West, providing a supply of cattle with which the growing consumption demands of the region can be met.

Declining Firm Concentration

The four largest meat packers in 1920—Swift, Armour, Wilson, and Cudahy—accounted for almost one-half of all commercial livestock slaughtering in the United States. They also controlled the major livestock terminals and almost the entire meat distribution system of the country which, at that time, consisted of wholesale branch houses and railroad car routes. The consent decree with the federal government in 1920 forced the major packers to dispose of some of their holdings and to limit the kinds of food handled by their wholesale establishments. The decree may have facilitated entry of new firms into the industry, although such a conclusion is certainly not obvious: the Big Four's share of livestock slaughtering was almost as large in 1947 as in 1920.[90]

The relative importance of the largest meat products firms has declined substantially since 1947. In that year, the four largest firms—Swift, Armour, Wilson and Morrell—accounted for 41 percent of production (value added) in meat packing; by 1963, that share had declined to 31 percent. In terms of employment, the four largest firms employed 47 percent of all meat packing workers in 1947 and 33 percent in 1963. The next four largest firms—Hormel, Hygrade, Oscar Mayer and Rath—employed only 10 percent of the industry's work force in 1963. Declining concentration has apparently continued to the present —a recent estimate put the Big Four share of meat packing sales at 25 percent.[91]

The reasons for the emergence of small firms, oriented toward local and regional markets, and the relative decline of the national packers may briefly be cited. First, entry to the industry has been facilitated by the development of direct buying by large retailers and by federal grading of meat. Direct buying from packers greatly reduced the necessary investment

---

[89] U.S. Bureau of Labor Statistics, *Industry Wage Survey, op. cit.,* p. 3.

[90] Arnould, *loc. cit.,* pp. 3-41.

[91] National Commission on Food Marketing, *op. cit.,* p. 8; Meyers, *loc. cit.*

in distribution facilities, and federal grading enabled small packers to compete with firms having established brand names. Second, there is some evidence which suggests that the optimal plant size in the industry has declined, making entry easier. Third, the large packers could not (or would not) readily adapt to the changing technology of the industry because they had considerable investments in older facilities which could not easily be disposed of. Furthermore, all of the large packers were unionized by 1947 and could not expect to gain significant wage advantages by moving to new locations. Thus, the way was open for small, low-cost operators to serve local and regional markets. Fourth, since 1947, the large meat packing firms have consistently reported net income after taxes at around 5 to 6 percent of net worth. Their rates of earnings have been among the lowest of all manufacturing industries and may have discouraged large packers from further investments in the meat industry. Armour, Swift, and Wilson have all made sizeable investments in nonfood enterprises in recent years, although in 1965 the four largest meat packers still derived 78 percent of their sales from meat and poultry products.[92]

The large firms have closed many more facilities than they have opened; between 1946 and 1965, the four largest closed 323 establishments, including branch houses, and opened only 73 new plants. Evidence on ease of entry is given by the fact that 842 firms entered meat packing in a three-year period after World War II. Exit is also easy; in the same period 548 firms left the industry.[93] As noted in Chapter 1, the meat industry has many small firms.

NEGRO EMPLOYMENT, *1950-1960*

Employment of Negroes in meat products declined slightly from 14.3 percent in 1950 to 13.8 percent in 1960 (Table 15, p. 54). It is likely that the employment losses in the industry during the 1950's had an adverse effect on the Negro share of employment. Falling total employment in the industry was accompanied by a decline in hiring new workers. In these cir-

---

[92] U.S. Department of Agriculture, *op. cit.*, pp. 266-267; National Commission on Food Marketing, *op. cit.*, pp. 12, 18-22, 59-70; Arnould, *loc. cit.*, pp. 73-78.

[93] National Commission on Food Marketing, *op. cit.*, p. 27; Arnould, *loc. cit.*, p. 69; *U.S. Census of Manufactures, 1963.*

cumstances, significant increases in the Negro proportions of
total employment were less likely to occur than under the conditions of an expanding work force, assuming that Negroes
would have comprised a large proportion of increments to employment, had they occurred.

Changes in the location of the meat industry appear to have
had an essentially neutral impact on the numbers of black workers employed, because job losses in the urban centers of the
North were offset by gains in the South. Total meat industry
employment in the North Central region fell by 2,619 between
1950 and 1960, but Negro employment declined by 6,118 (Table
15). The difference in these two figures reflects the fact that
during the 1950's meat industry employment in the North Central region was not only declining, but was also shifting out of
urban centers, where many Negroes lived, to cornbelt locations,
where the available labor supply was almost entirely white.
Negro employment in the Chicago, Kansas City, and St. Louis
meat packing centers fell by almost 7,000 in the 1950's (Table
18). Over 80 percent of these job losses occurred in Chicago
alone. It is noteworthy that the closings of the Chicago facilities of the major packers came at a time when these firms, for a
variety of reasons, were experiencing difficulties in hiring white
workers. Writing in 1953 about the supply of labor to the Chicago Swift plant, where 55 percent of production workers were
then black, Purcell stated:

> . . . It is most likely that Negroes, victims of limited edu-
> cational opportunities and persisting discrimination in craft
> work and office work, will bear the brunt of the [manual]
> labor for many years to come. . . . The continued high
> employment of Negroes and the refusal of whites to work
> in the plant may make the plant community virtually a seg-
> regated Negro community. . . .

> . . . If Swift Chicago wishes to retain a sizeable proportion
> of white workers, it will have to improve working condi-
> tions, raise wages, and above all improve its community
> relations in conjunction with the other packers of the Chi-
> cago yards with whom (perhaps unfairly) it is joined in
> the popular mind.[94]

---

[94] Purcell, *Worker Speaks, op. cit.,* p. 30.

Whether labor supply considerations were significant in the decisions to close the Chicago facilities cannot be determined—certainly other cost factors were more important. It is clear, however, that many Negro workers lost their jobs when these facilities were closed.

TABLE 18. *Meat Industry*
Total and Negro Employment, Four Urban Centers
1950 and 1960

	Total		Negro		Percent Negro	
	1950	1960	1950	1960	1950	1960
Chicago	35,143	19,421	10,072	4,553	28.7	23.4
Greater Kansas City	8,208	5,567	2,568	2,141	31.3	38.4
Omaha	9,654	9,131	1,620	1,722	16.8	18.8
St. Louis (includes East St. Louis)	10,389	7,453	2,700	1,935	26.0	26.0
Total	63,394	41,570	16,960	10,350	26.7	24.9
Percent of industry employment	23.1	13.1	43.3	23.6		

Source: *U. S. Census of Population:*

1950, Vol. II, *Characteristics of the Population*, State Volumes, Table 83.

1960, PC (1) D, *Detailed Characteristics*, State Volumes, Table 129.

In the South, on the other hand, Negro employment increased by almost 9,000 during the 1950's (Table 15, p. 54) so that by 1960 that region employed one-half of all black workers in the industry (Table 16), and the Negro share of employment was much larger in the South than in other regions (Table 15). The Negro share of employment in the North Central region, still the leading location for the meat industry, declined from 14.2 to 10.4 percent between 1950 and 1960.

The regional redistribution of employment did not have a neutral impact on the wage level of jobs held by Negroes, however. Since so much of the industry expansion in the South occurred in poultry processing, most Negro job gains were in that division of the industry. The precise gains cannot be given because data on Negro employment are not separately available for the poultry processing segment of the meat packing sector. Moreover, as noted in Chapter 2, Table 9, page 15, average weekly earnings in the poultry division were only approximately one-half those in meat packing in 1968. Thus the transfer of employment from meat packing to poultry processing had an adverse effect on Negro wages and incomes. Even within the meat packing division, the regional shift of Negro employment from North to South lowered the average wage of jobs held by black workers because of the substantial wage differential between these two regions.

The shift of Negro employment from meat packing to poultry processing also involved an increase in the employment of Negro women relative to Negro men because of the prominence of women in the latter division of the meat industry. (Again, the data to quantatively support this conclusion are not available.) More than one-half of all employees in poultry processing are women compared to only 15 percent in meat packing (Table 8, p. 14). The significance of this greater employment of women is disclosed by the fact that women accounted for three-fourths of the 4,800 increase which occurred in Negro meat industry employment between 1950 and 1960.

The effects of diminishing concentration in the meat industry on Negro employment are not clear. Data for 1966, for example, which will be discussed in subsequent pages, disclose a slightly lower representation of black workers in the eight largest firms than in all others; it might be concluded from this finding that the decline in concentration did not have a significant impact on Negro employment. On the other hand, if the large firms had retained their earlier proportions of industry employment and also their large metropolitan facilities, Negro employment in meat products would certainly be greater than it is today. But movement of plants away from Chicago, Kansas City, and other large cities would have occurred even if the large firms had retained their earlier percentages of industry output and employment. Movement of meat packing into Iowa and Minnesota, not a decline in the relative size of the large firms, was the fundamental factor in the reduction of Negro employment which occurred in the North Central region.

In concluding this section, it may be noted that the trends of the 1950's have continued. Because of the dislocations, Negro employment today in the meat packing sector of the meat industry—once the scene of very tumultuous events in the history of labor and race relations in the United States—is probably lower than at any time since the late 1930's.

NEGROES AND MEAT INDUSTRY UNIONS, *1930-1960*

Passage of the National Industrial Recovery Act in 1933 and the National Labor Relations Act in 1935 stimulated union organizing activity in the meat industry. Against the strong resistance of the major packers, the Amalgamated—then the only union attempting to organize a major proportion of industry employees—was, however, able to achieve recognition and actual collective bargaining in only a few plants. Then, in October 1937, the Congress of Industrial Organizations (CIO), which had just previously achieved spectacular successes in organizing the steel and automobile industries, established the Packinghouse Workers Organizing Committee (PWOC) to compete with the Amalgamated in organizing the meat industry. Van Bittner, a CIO official, was named chairman of the PWOC, with Don Harris of the Hosiery Workers as national director. Some months later, Henry Johnson, a Negro, became assistant national director.[95]

The U.S. Supreme Court decision in April 1937, which established the constitutional legality of the National Labor Relations Act, provided much needed help to the Amalgamated and the PWOC, while at the same time dooming the existence of the packers' employee representation committees. These committees, which had been sponsored by the packers in the 1920's as their version of collective bargaining, were made illegal by the NLRA. A number of independent local unions did develop from the outlawed employee representation groups, however. Thus, by late 1937 a three-cornered contest to organize packinghouse workers had begun, with independent local unions, the Amalgamated, and the PWOC all competing for the support of the workers. Ultimately, many of the independent unions were defeated in elections or were found to be company-dominated by the National Labor Relations Board. They were, however, certified as bargaining representatives in a number of Swift plants and, as the National Brotherhood of Packinghouse Workers, have continued to hold bargaining rights in six major Swift plants up to the present.

Most of the successes in meat packing went to the PWOC, which in 1943 became the United Packinghouse Workers of America (UPWA). Brody estimated that by 1944, the UPWA represented about 60 percent of the workers in the industry, the

---

[95] Brody, *op. cit.*, Chapter 8; Kampfert, *loc. cit.*

Amalgamated about 20 percent, and the Brotherhood about 7 percent. The UPWA obtained bargaining rights at most of the large plants in the industry, the Amalgamated won in many small firms and small establishments of the major packers, and the Brotherhood became bargaining representative in some of the Swift plants.[96]

The PWOC received an enthusiastic reception from most packinghouse workers because of their disillusionment over previous abortive attempts of the Amalgamated to organize the industry, the dramatic success of the CIO in organizing other industries, and the belief that the PWOC would, and the Amalgamated would not, use an industrial rather than craft basis of organization. In fact, by the late 1930's officials of the Amalgamated were convinced that effective unionization could not be built around a separate union for each distinct occupational group in the meat industry, and they were only slightly less committed to the industrial form of organization than was the PWOC.[97]

The fact that the PWOC had much more success than the Amalgamated in organizing Negroes probably had little to do with the generally greater organizing achievements of the former. In the late 1930's, not more than 15 to 25 percent of the bargaining unit workers in northern meat packing, where almost all of the unionization took place, were black. Negroes were almost nonexistent in the interior centers (of Iowa and Minnesota), such as Cedar Rapids and Austin, where the PWOC obtained some of its earliest success. The initial, racially equalitarian policies of the PWOC did reap large dividends during World War II, however, when the Negro fraction of UPWA membership rose to one-third.[98]

But even though Negroes were a rather small fraction of packinghouse workers in the late 1930's, past experience had made it clear that they had to be organized to assure viable collective bargaining in meat packing. There can be no doubt that the PWOC and its successor, the UPWA, worked much harder at that aspect of organizing and did much more to translate

---

[96] Brody, *op. cit.*, Chapter 9.

[97] *Ibid.*, p. 174.

[98] John Hope II, *Equality of Opportunity* (Washington: Public Affairs Press, 1956), p. 101. Although Hope's data appear to pertain to 1948, interviews with UPWA officials in the summer of 1968 indicated that the basis of his estimates was information provided by the War Manpower Commission and thus the data apply to the World War II years.

rhetoric into action than did the Amalgamated. Although Amalgamated officials were aware of the need to organize Negroes and employed several black organizers for this purpose, according to Brody, they refused to "crusade on the race issue" while the UPWA had no such inhibitions.[99] Others have been more critical of Amalgamated relations with black workers. One study asserted that, before the PWOC appeared on the scene, "The [Amalgamated] union resisted most attempts to allow Negroes to be more than dues paying and almost non-participating members."[100]

Whether "crusade" is the appropriate term, the PWOC and UPWA did give vigorous support both to nonracial grievances involving black workers and to the elimination of discrimination. For example, in 1938 an Armour local in Kansas City affiliated with the PWOC struck for several days over the company's refusal to pay a total of $22.09 to six Negro workers for wages lost during the arbitration of a grievance.[101] The UPWA also militantly objected to plant practices which discriminated against Negroes per se, such as "tagging" their time cards and excluding them from plant departments visited by the public.[102]

This kind of plant-level activism for fair and equal treatment was the most important element in the successful organizing of Negroes by the UPWA. In addition, the favorable racial image of the CIO helped the PWOC and UPWA with organizing black workers. Henry Johnson, as assistant director of the PWOC, had great appeal for Negro workers in the meat industry and was able to persuade many to become members of local PWOC affiliates.[103] Finally, the UPWA's endorsement of black community groups and their goals won for the union sympathetic support from the National Association for the Advancement of Colored People, the National Urban League and other organizations, aiding efforts to organize black workers.[104]

The UPWA continued (to the present) militantly to pursue equal rights for all members after collective bargaining in the

---

[99] Brody, *op. cit.*, p .176.

[100] Horace R. Cayton and George S. Mitchell, *Black Workers and the New Unions* (Chapel Hill: University of North Carolina Press, 1939), p. 272.

[101] Kampfert, *loc. cit.*, Part IV, p. 124.

[102] *Ibid.*, Part IV.

[103] Interviews with officials of UPWA, June 1968.

[104] Ray Marshall, *The Negro and Organized Labor* (New York: John Wiley & Sons, 1965), pp. 39-41; Brody, *op. cit.*, p. 177.

industry was well established. "No union operating in the South," according to Marshall, "has followed a more militantly equalitarian racial position than the UPWA." [105] The same statement applies equally well to the North. Nondiscrimination clauses covering hiring as well as conditions of employment were negotiated in all UPWA agreements. Elimination of segregated plant facilities was pressed. Based partly on a unique self-survey of members' attitudes, educational programs emphasizing the union's antidiscrimination position were conducted. A financial contribution was made by the UPWA to the Southern Christian Leadership Conference in 1957, even before its director, Martin Luther King, Jr., had achieved national prominence.[106] Community fair employment practice and equal rights programs in the North were consistently supported by local and district UPWA leaders. All of these things were done during the 1940's and 1950's, when it had not yet become so fashionable for social and business institutions to be actively concerned with minority rights.

One of the most important UPWA efforts on behalf of minority groups was the filing of grievances alleging discrimination at one of Swift's Chicago plants in 1950.[107] The grievance action was aimed at enforcement of a provision of the collective agreement which prohibited discrimination in hiring. The union, after sending several white and black women to apply for plant jobs, charged that Swift was discriminating against the latter. The grievance finally went to the nationally known arbitrator, Ralph Seward, who found Swift in violation of the contract. Seward stated that "the Company was not only failing to give Negro applicants 'fair and reasonable consideration,' it was failing to give them any consideration whatsoever." The award, in this case, brought employment, back pay, and retroactive seniority to thirteen Negro women. Although the action was taken against Swift, it had implications for much of the industry. As will be discussed later, discrimination by the major packers against employing Negro women had long been suspected, though never proved. Following the arbitration award, there was an increase in the amount of centralized control exerted by the major packers over plant hiring practices in order to prevent similar occurrences. The UPWA has made similar attempts to increase

---

[105] Marshall, *op. cit.*, p. 179.

[106] United Packinghouse Workers of America, *Constitutional Convention, Officer Reports*, 1957, pp. 56-58.

[107] *Labor Arbitration Reports*, 1952, Vol. 17, pp. 537-540.

the white collar employment of Negroes—acting under fair employment practice laws and antidiscrimination provisions of government contracts—but it has achieved only token change in this area.

The vigorous pursuit of equal rights for Negroes brought some problems to the UPWA (although, on balance, the union racial policies brought it more gains than losses). Majority status for Negroes in a large Swift local in Chicago and the movement of its union business office into a Negro neighborhood had the effect of substantially reducing participation in the union by white members.[108] Several stockhandlers' locals disaffiliated rather than accept Negro members. Attempts to desegregate plant facilities in the South were in some instances, strongly resisted by white members; a Swift local in Moultrie, Georgia, joined the Amalgamated rather than submit to integration of plant facilities. Whites withdrew from a number of southern locals, leaving these locals with predominantly black membership.[109]

In part, the southern reaction to the UPWA equalitarian policies of the 1940's and 1950's was directed to Communist influence within the union. Knowing that a number of Communists held local and district positions of leadership, many white southerners (and probably some northerners as well) found it easy to attribute the racial policies of the union completely to Communist influence, which in turn provided them with a moral rationalization for resisting these policies.[110]

The other major meat industry union, the Amalgamated, has long practiced antidiscrimination policies at the national level, and its officials have often spoken out in support of equal rights for minority persons.[111] It has not, however, been nearly as vigorous as the UPWA in its implementation of these policies. One reason for this may have been the smaller percentage of members who are Negro—probably less than 15 percent in the early 1960's, compared to about 25 percent for the UPWA. The sizeable number of retail food store members in the Amalgamated has probably also restrained antidiscrimination activity in comparison with the UPWA. The major food chains historically

---

[108] Purcell, *Worker Speaks, op. cit.,* pp. 64-72.

[109] Marshall, *op. cit.,* pp. 180-181.

[110] *Ibid.*

[111] The UPWA by 1960 had five Negroes on its executive board; the Amalgamated, one.

did not employ Negroes in the meat departments of stores with predominantly white customers, and there is no evidence that Amalgamated retail locals have seriously objected to this practice.[112] A third reason for the less active antidiscrimination practices of the Amalgamated may be in the tradition and structure of the union. It was founded and long dominated by skilled butchers, who had a strong preference for local control of union activities in the craft tradition. Thus, the Amalgamated, in great contrast to the UPWA's strong (some would say heavy-handed) centralized control, did not attempt to pressure its local affiliates into vigorous antidiscrimination activity. Attempts to do so would have met with little success, although some Amalgamated locals were instrumental in desegregating plant facilities. All this is not to imply that the Amalgamated has not been concerned with racially equalitarian practices in the meat industry; merely that it suffers in comparison with the UPWA. Indeed, it may be noted that Amalgamated support of federal civil rights legislation has been sufficient to get it placed on lists of "enemy" organizations prepared by White Citizens' Councils.[113]

Although both major unions in the meat industry have been vigorous—compared with other unions—in their support of equal treatment of minority members, this does not mean that equal treatment has everywhere been obtained. Officials of both the UPWA and the Amalgamated admit that segregated union meetings or social functions may occur without their knowledge, especially in the South. Segregated activities have been less likely in the UPWA than in the Amalgamated because of the greater efforts of the former to implement its equalitarian policies; but even the UPWA probably was not able to eliminate completely the influence of its racist white members. That a significant number of such members exists is suggested by the 15 percent support received by George Wallace in Presidential straw balloting conducted among UPWA members in the spring of 1968.[114]

---

[112] Very recently, Amalgamated locals in Detroit and New York have taken affirmative action to help to recruit Negro butchers for supermarkets. Our study of supermarkets, now in progress in the Racial Policies of American Industry series, will show, however, that Negroes are rare in such jobs and that the retail butchers' locals have been quite exclusionist.

[113] Marshall, *op. cit.*, p. 196.

[114] *The Packinghouse Worker* (May 1968), p. 12.

In spite of some lingering racial prejudice among their memberships, the meat industry unions have eliminated discrimination within their locals, as far as an outside observer can tell, and have had an enormous influence on the removal of discrimination within the employee units for which they bargain.

In recent years, the two major unions in the industry have cooperated in collective bargaining and gradually, as a result, relations between them have grown warmer. Moreover, the move of the major packing plants from central city locations resulted in considerable diminution in the membership of the UPWA. These factors led in 1968 to a merger of the two unions with the Amalgamated as the surviving organization. It is possible that the merger could result in better treatment of minority members if UPWA ideology and expertise in this area are spread throughout the industry. It does appear that former UPWA officers will have major responsibility for administering the meat packing division of the new union. Whether the merger could also hasten the unionization of many black workers in the southern part of the meat industry, including the rapidly growing poultry division, remains also to be seen.

As an addendum to this chapter, it may be noted that the practice of using minority group workers to combat unionism did not completely disappear from the meat industry, even in the 1960's. In October 1967, 17 men of Latin-American origin recruited from California were brought to Harlan, Iowa, a small town in the western part of the state, where a newly organized local of the UPWA was on strike against the Western Iowa Pork Company. Late on a Sunday evening, when these men attempted to move into house trailers on company grounds, they were attacked by pickets and a small-scale riot followed, causing $20,000 damage to company property. Local law enforcement officials made little effort to stop the violence. The impact of this event on racial attitudes in western Iowa is unknown.[115] More recently, Mexican-Americans have been utilized to replace strikers in a bitter contest between the Amalgamated and Iowa Beef Packers which began at the latter's Dakota, Nebraska plant.

---

[115] Donald E. Whistler, "The Involvement of Governor Harold E. Hughes in Three Labor Disputes," Master's thesis, Department of Economics, Iowa State University, 1967, pp. 41-45.

CHAPTER V.

Negro Employment in the 1960's

The principal trends of the previous decades continued in the meat industry during the 1960's. Data strictly comparable to the Census of Population are, of course, as yet unavailable, but sufficient data are available from our field research to affirm that continued decentralization of meat packing away from the large cities and centers of Negro population has been offset by the growth of the southern poultry industry and by the impact of labor shortages and civil rights pressures. As a result, Negro employment in the meat industry has remained at a relatively constant ratio since 1950. On the other hand, the center of Negro employment has continued to move from meat packing in the North to poultry in the South.

FACTORS AFFECTING NEGRO EMPLOYMENT

Data were obtained for 1964, 1966, and 1968, but since those for 1966 were the most complete, that year's sample will be used for much of our analysis. For 1966, our sample includes about 50 percent of the industry's employment, and all of the ten largest firms, which account for about 70 percent of our sample. As in our 1964 and 1968 samples, our 1966 data underrepresent the small firms.

The Negro's Share of Employment, 1966

In 1966, 14.4 percent of the meat industry's employees were black (Table 19). The 1960 figure, according to the census of that year, was 13.8 percent. Census data are based upon responses from individuals; our sample used employer payroll data. There are also other differences, but the closeness of the percentages for 1966 and 1960 (as well as 1950 when, according to the census, it was 14.3 percent) makes it reasonable to conclude that the share of meat industry employment held by Negroes has been stable for some time. Although the Negro share of total employment appears not to be changing, shifts in

Negro employment among various divisions of the industry are undoubtedly continuing. The major shift, described in the previous chapter, is from meat packing to poultry processing, as employment falls in the former and increases in the latter. From 1962 to 1967, employment fell by 11,000 (5.6 percent) in meat packing and rose by 17,000 (24.2 percent) in poultry processing.[116] If employment continues to grow more rapidly in poultry processing than in the entire industry, a slow increase in the Negro share of industry employment can be expected. The reason for this is that most of the growth in the poultry industry is occurring in the South, where black laborers continue to be more readily available than in the North. Data in the author's possession show that many poultry firms in the South employ production work forces which are almost completely Negro, although some reverse this practice and do not employ any black workers.[117]

TABLE 19.   *Meat Industry*

Total and Negro Employment by Region
1966

Location	Total	Negro	Percent Negro
Northeast	10,670	1,420	13.3
North Central	88,770	9,360	10.5
South	36,050	9,610	26.7
West	13,110	1,030	7.9
U.S. Total	148,600	21,430	14.4
Standard Metropolitan Statistical Areas	98,080	14,200	14.5
Other	50,520	7,230	14.3

Source: Data in the author's possession.

Note: For regional definitions, see Table 4 p. 9.

---

[116] U.S. Bureau of Labor Statistics, *Employment and Earnings, 1909-1968*, *op. cit.*, pp. 461-469.

[117] The poultry establishments of the four largest meat packers in 1964 employed a work force of which Negroes comprised 24 percent; this compares with a Negro percentage of 13 in all plants of these four firms. Sixty percent of all Negro employees in the poultry operations were female, compared to an 11 percent female proportion of Negro employment in all plants of the four largest firms (from data in the possession of the author).

Women and Other Minorities

A sex breakdown for the data in Table 19 is not available, but 1968 figures for the industry's ten largest firms are shown in Table 20. Negro males are better represented in these large firms than are Negro females. On the other hand, the latter have made substantial progress since 1940 when Negroes were only 2.5 percent of female employment in the industry (Appendix Table A-1).

TABLE 20.　*Meat Industry*

Total and Minority Group Employment by Sex,
In the Ten Largest Firms
1968

	Employment			Percent of Total Employment		
	Male & Female	Male	Female	Male & Female	Male	Female
Total	118,987	98,676	20,311			
Negro	12,998	11,236	1,762	10.9	11.4	8.7
Spanish-American	4,985	4,115	870	4.2	4.2	4.3
Total Minority[a]	18,466	15,715	2,751	15.5	15.9	13.5

Source: Data in the author's possession.

[a] Includes American Indians and Orientals.

Table 20 also shows that "Spanish-Americans," (mostly Mexicans) comprised over 4 percent of employment in the meat industry in 1968. Most Mexicans were employed in plants in the Southwest, but significant numbers also worked in such midwestern locations as Kansas City and Omaha. (A study of the problems of Mexican-Americans in the industry might well be worth a separate monograph.)

Regional Variations

Negroes are now much better represented in the southern sector of the meat industry than in the North. The South employed only approximately one-fourth of all employees in our 1966 sample, but still accounted for almost one-half of all black workers included in the survey. (See Table 19.) Negroes in 1966 comprised between 8 and 13 percent of meat industry employment in the three northern regions of the United States, compared to nearly 27 percent in the South. Once more it should be noted that poultry establishments, low wages, non-union firms, and a large female proportion of the work force are much more charactcristic of the meat industry in the South than in the North.

In contrast to the South, employment of Negroes in the Midwest—still the leading region of the meat industry, especially for meat packing—is very low. In 1966 black workers were less than 3 percent of all employees in the two leading meat industry states—Iowa and Minnesota.

Somewhat surprisingly, meat establishments located in metropolitan areas do not employ a significantly larger percentage of Negroes than establishments in nonmetropolitan locations on a nationwide basis. However, if we were able to make this comparison for the North and South separately, some differences would no doubt show up. (See Table 21 for Midwest.) Relatively few Negroes are available for employment in nonmetropolitan establishments of the North, but this is not the case in the South.

TABLE 21. *Meat Industry*
Total and Negro Employment in Four Large Urban Areas
and Six Small Cities
1966

	Total	Negro	Percent Negro
Four large urban areas: Chicago, Kansas City, Omaha, and St. Louis	23,550	5,600	23.8
Six small cities: Austin, Minnesota; Cedar Rapids, Ottumwa, and Waterloo, Iowa; Madison, Wisconsin; and Sioux Falls, South Dakota	20,320	400	2.0

Source: Data in the author's possession.

The very sharp contrast which exists in the North between employment of Negroes in large urban meat centers and in the smaller citics which contain meat plants is shown in Table 21. The four traditional centers of the industry, all large cities, employed 5,600 Negroes in 1966. This was 23.8 percent of industry employment in these locations (as a result of plant closings, both Negro and total employment in these four locations is now

well below that of 1966). Six small midwestern cities, all of
which contain meat plants employing at least 2,500 persons, employed only 400 black workers or just 2.0 percent of total employment. St. Paul, Minnesota is one large urban center of the
meat industry which does not employ many black workers. Only
4 percent of its 6,200 meat packing workers were Negro in
1966.[118]

Plant Size

Employment of Negroes in establishments of varying size is
shown in Table 22. The smallest black share of employment is in
the largest plants and the largest share is in relatively small
plants. No conclusions about the relation between plant size and
Negro employment can be drawn from these figures, however.
The low employment of Negroes in the large plants is a result
of the small-city midwestern location of almost all of these
plants, and location in the South may be the reason for the large
Negro share of employment in plants which employ 100-249
workers. Black workers are employed in significant numbers in
plants of all sizes in the meat industry; the precise numbers
depend in large part on the size of Negro representation in the
labor market which the plant draws upon.

TABLE 22. *Meat Industry*

Total and Negro Employment by Plant Size
1966

| Plant Size (Employees) | Employment | | |
	Total	Negro	Percent Negro
Less than 100	11,620	1,360	11.7
100-249	23,790	4,420	18.6
250-499	29,660	4,570	15.4
500-999	26,090	4,970	19.1
1,000 and over	57,440	6,110	10.6

Source: Data in the author's possession.

---

[118] Swift is in the process of closing most of its St. Paul plant which will
reduce employment in that area's meat industry substantially. (*Business
Week*, August 30, 1969, p. 84.)

Company Differences

Large differences in the Negro percent of employment exist among the various firms in the meat industry. It appears that these variations are due in great measure to differences in the racial composition of the cities in which the firms have their plants.

One broad difference is that which exists between the largest firms and the rest of the industry. Our data show that in 1966, the Negro share of employment was 11.2 percent in the ten largest firms and 20.8 percent in all others. This major difference exists chiefly because the plants operated by the ten largest firms are located predominantly in lightly populated areas of the Midwest, where few blacks live, while many of the other firms are located in the South.

Considerable variation is also found among these ten largest firms. In one, 23 percent of the work force is made up of Negroes. At the other extreme is a firm in which blacks comprise only one percent of all workers.

An attempt was made through multiple regression analysis to determine if there are company differences in willingness to employ Negroes once the influence of the Negro percentage of the local labor force is accounted for. The results of this failed to show any significant (statistical or otherwise) differences, although they are not conclusive since less than one-third of the variation in the Negro percentage of establishment employment (the dependent variable) was accounted for by the variables available for this analysis.

Summary: Significance of Location

In summary then, location appears to be by far the most important influence on Negro representation in plant work forces. Generally, plants located in areas where Negroes are a sizeable fraction of the population will have a sizeable fraction of black workers in their work forces. There are many exceptions to this generalization, and there is no discernible explanation for the exceptions. Racial attitudes of plant owners, managers, and white workers, no doubt, influence Negro employment, as do many other factors. Yet, even attitudes do not have a predictable influence, as would seem to be evidenced by the employment of blacks in substantial numbers in many southern meat plants.

OVER-ALL TRENDS, *1964-1968*

In our sample survey, data on Negro and total employment were obtained for 252 meat establishments, including most large plants in the industry, for 1966 and 1968. For 1964, the data were available for only 205 establishments, although as in the two years later, most large plants were included. These data, shown in Table 23, permit an examination of changes in Negro employment during the 1960's, with reasonable comparability between 1964 and the two later years, and full comparability between 1966 and 1968.

Negro employment in the industry did increase between 1964 and 1968. The more precise comparison of 1966 with 1968 shows a gain of almost 1,500 black workers and an increase in the Negro share of employment of about one percentage point. Employment gains occurred for both Negro men and women. However, the Negro share of female employment increased more rapidly than did the Negro share of male employment. The former has apparently risen substantially since 1964.

Examination of the regional data indicates that most of the gains in Negro employment (and in total employment) occurred in the South. As previously indicated, the poultry division of the meat industry has been growing rapidly in the South. Employment in the 92 southern establishments which the data cover rose by 2,353 between 1966 and 1968 and blacks obtained almost 60 percent of this increase. Negro employment remained quite stable in the other regions. Some gains were made in the Northeast and West, but these regions do not contain many meat industry employees. The major region for the industry, the North Central, experienced no significant change in either total or Negro employment between 1966 and 1968. It did, however, experience a slight shift of employment from males to females for both black and white workers.

There is no way to assign causation for the recent slight increases in Negro employment in the meat industry. In particular, it cannot be determined whether all or part of the gains resulted from public policies for equal employment opportunity or would have occurred even in the absence of these policies. But the best guess is the latter, based on the fact that the Negro employment gains occurred in small and middle-sized firms in the South, where Negroes by 1960 had already obtained a substantial share of meat industry employment. It is likely that, at the relatively low wages paid by southern meat estab-

TABLE 23. *Meat Industry*

Total and Negro Employment in the United States by Sex and Region 1964, 1966, 1968

	All Employees			Male			Female		
	Total	Negro	Percent Negro	Total	Negro	Percent Negro	Total	Negro	Percent Negro
United States									
1964[a]	105,023	13,890	13.2	83,618	11,452	13.7	21,405	2,428	11.3
1966[b]	110,834	14,925	13.5	88,691	11,949	13.5	22,143	2,976	13.4
1968[c]	113,299	16,356	14.4	89,552	12,603	14.1	23,747	3,753	15.8
Northeast									
1964	5,001	559	11.2	4,081	517	12.7	920	42	4.3
1966	6,372	835	13.1	5,050	673	13.3	1,322	162	12.1
1968	6,311	927	14.7	4,939	751	15.2	1,372	176	13.1
North Central									
1964	68,834	8,068	11.7	57,023	7,228	12.7	11,811	840	7.1
1966	71,269	7,139	10.0	59,723	6,547	11.0	11,546	592	5.1
1968	71,284	7,086	9.9	59,253	6,371	10.8	12,031	715	6.0
South									
1964	22,175	4,582	20.6	15,373	3,068	20.0	6,802	1,514	22.2
1966	25,522	6,413	25.1	17,665	4,221	23.9	7,857	2,192	27.9
1968	27,875	7,769	27.9	19,006	4,963	26.1	8,869	2,806	31.7
West									
1964	9,013	671	7.4	7,141	639	9.0	1,872	32	1.6
1966	7,671	538	7.0	6,253	508	8.2	1,418	30	2.1
1968	7,829	574	7.3	6,354	518	8.2	1,475	56	3.7

Source: Data in the author's possession.

Note: For regional definitions, see Table 4, p. 9.

[a] 205 establishments.   [b] 252 establishments.   [c] 252 establishments.

lishments, employment of an increasing number of black workers is dictated by conditions of labor supply because adequate
numbers of qualified whites are not available. Many of the blacks
who are being hired are women employed in poultry plants.

It is worth noting that both Negro employment and the Negro
share of total employment declined in the meat industry's four
largest firms between 1964 and 1968. The employment data for
these four firms are shown in Table 24. During this four-year
interval, the four largest meat packers reduced their employment
of all males by 1,300 and increased their employment of all females by 1,000. Three-fourths of the decline in male employment fell to black workers. These occurrences are consistent
with movement away from the older metropolitan centers of the
industry, and several plants were closed in such areas between
1964 and 1968.

TABLE 24. *Meat Industry*

Total and Negro Employment, Four Largest Firms
1964 and 1968

	Total	Negro	Percent Negro
1964	87,410	11,430	13.1
1968	87,150	10,510	12.1

Source: Data in the author's possession.

OCCUPATIONAL STATUS

Negro employment remained fairly steady in the meat industry between 1950 and 1968, but substantial changes occurred in
the location and nature of Negro employment during this period.
What of the occupational status? To determine whether, as one
would assume, the occupational distribution of black workers in
the meat industry improved as the time span of their employment increased, we shall review their occupational status since
the turn of the century before analyzing the current situation.

The 1910-1940 Period

Almost 98 percent of the Negroes employed in meat packing
in 1910 were low-skilled manual workers—either laborers or operatives—while 76.3 percent of all workers were low skilled
(Table 25). Almost three-quarters of the Negro employees were
in the lowest skill classification—laborers—compared to less than
one-half of all workers. Very few of the 5,810 black workers
in the industry were in skilled manual positions: 90 were fore-

men or skilled craftsmen—carpenters, machinists, plumbers, etc. Even fewer—only 40—held nonmanual (white collar) jobs, mostly as clerks.

The low level of jobs held by black workers at that time is not necessarily an indication of inequitable treatment or limited skills. Most Negroes who were working in the meat industry in 1910 had not been so employed for very long.

The census of population for 1920 enumerated meat industry employment only for the operative and laborer classifications (Table 25). Among Negroes, there were nearly three laborers for every operative, while the ratio was less than two to one for all workers. As mentioned earlier, meat industry employment expanded sharply in the war decade of 1910-20, most of it in the laborer rather than operative classification. About three-fourths of the increase in Negro employment during the decade took place in this classification, compared to less than two-thirds of the increase in total employment.

TABLE 25. *Meat Industry*
Occupational Distribution of Total and Negro Employment
1910-1940

Occupation	1910 Total	1910 Negro	1920 Total	1920 Negro	1930 Total	1930 Negro	1940 Total	1940 Negro a
Nonmanual	15,720	40	n.a.	n.a.	44,350	220	57,060	200
Craft and foreman	9,200	90	n.a.	n.a.	13,300	270	14,310	170
Operative	25,900	1,600	49,990	7,600	61,300	7,810	93,710	7,120
Laborerb	33,900	3,100	59,550	14,700	46,000	10,120	45,050	5,050
Stockyard laborer	6,000	540	22,890	6,030	17,800	2,300	—	—
Otherc	3,640	440	—	—	—	—	—	—
All occupations	94,360	5,810	132,430	28,330	182,750	20,720	210,130	12,540
			Percent of Employment					
Nonmanual	16.7	0.7			24.3	1.1	27.2	1.6
Craft and foreman	9.7	1.5			7.3	1.3	6.8	1.3
Operative	27.4	27.5			33.5	37.7	44.6	56.8
Laborer	35.9	53.4			25.2	48.8	21.4	40.3
Stockyard laborer	6.4	9.3			9.7	11.1	—	—
Other	3.9	7.6			—	—	—	—
	100.0	100.0			100.0	100.0	100.0	100.0

Sources: *U.S. Census of Population,* various years; Alba M. Edwards, *A Social-Economic Grouping of the Gainful Workmen of the United States* (Washington: Government Printing Office, 1938), Table 31, p. 98.

a Data available only for the South and thirteen large northern cities. Includes 77% of 1940 Negro employment in the meat industry.

b Includes a small number of service workers in 1930 and 1940.

c Includes all who could not be placed into one of the other categories from the occupational classifications used for the 1910 census.

The Chicago Commission on Race Relations, based on its investigations conducted in 1920, reported numerous complaints from black workers about job assignments and lack of promotions in the meat industry of Chicago. The Commission stated: "There are no Negro foremen over mixed gangs. The highest position a Negro is able to reach is that of sub-foreman over a group of Negro workmen." [119]

By 1930 low-skilled jobs had declined to 68.4 percent of all meat industry employment, but 97.6 percent of all black workers were still in these jobs—the same percentage as in 1910 (Table 25). Black representation in skilled jobs was abysmally low: of 3,300 stenographers and typists in the industry, two were Negro, as were 11 of 7,000 salesmen; 47 Negroes held foreman positions and a little over 200 worked as skilled craftsmen. Certainly some, perhaps most, of the Negroes who held white collar and skilled manual jobs worked in local, Negro-owned firms in the South. In short, in 1930, blacks in the meat industry were almost completely absent from jobs above the semi-skilled level.

The meat industry had employed a significant number of Negroes for more than twenty years by 1930. Particularly during the 1920's, following the great expansion of Negro employment from 1916 to 1920, movement of blacks into the more skilled occupations should, under normal assumptions of progress, have occurred. It did not, however. In that era of employee relations, characterized in large meat packing firms as well as large firms generally, by employee representation committees and paternalistic personnel programs, the job level of black workers in the meat industry was not raised.

Data compiled from the 1930 census of population by Alba M. Edwards permit comparison of the meat packing occupations held by Negroes and other populations. Table 26, calculated for male workers, shows that a smaller percentage of Negroes than Mexicans were in the lowest skill classification. About 3,500 of the latter were employed in the meat industry in 1930; they had first entered the industry in World War I, and were still employed predominately as laborers in 1930.[120] Foreign-born whites,

---

[119] Chicago Commission on Race Relations, *op. cit.*, pp. 389-390.

[120] The 1930 census of population was the only one that enumerated Mexicans separately until the Spanish surname enumerations for five southwestern states became available in 1950 and 1960. The Edwards data for 1930 combine Mexicans and Orientals, but very few of the latter were employed in meat packing.

however, were more frequently employed at the higher occupational levels than were Negroes—about 20 percent of the former were in skilled craft and nonmanual jobs. Native-born whites enjoyed the best occupational status, although one-half of this population was in low-skilled employment.

TABLE 26. *Meat Industry*

Occupational Percentage Distribution of Male Employment
Selected Populations
1930

Occupation	Total	Native White	Foreign-Born White	Negro	Mexicans[a]
Professional and managerial	5.0%	6.7%	3.2%	— %	0.2%
Clerical and sales	21.0	30.0	7.9	1.2	2.6
Craft and foreman	9.1	10.6	9.7	1.5	2.0
Operatives	35.6	31.4	45.7	40.7	26.5
Unskilled	29.3	21.3	33.5	56.6	68.7
	100.0	100.0	100.0	100.0	100.0

Source: Alba M. Edwards, *A Social-Economic Grouping of the Gainful Workers of the United States* (Washington: Government Printing Office, 1938), Table 31, p. 98.

[a] Includes a small percentage of other races.

Two-thirds of all women and almost all Negro women employed in the meat industry in 1930 were in low-skilled manual jobs. Most of the women who held clerical positions were native-born whites, but a majority of this group as well was employed in manual work. Ten percent of the foreign-born white women were clerical workers, while only one percent of the black women were in clerical positions.

The depression decade of the 1930's saw the continued virtual exclusion of black workers from the skilled occupations of the meat industry; in 1940, 97.1 percent of all Negroes were still employed in low-skilled manual jobs (Table 25). Although Negroes experienced a rapid shift from laborer to operative jobs between 1930 and 1940, this did not provide them with any relative gain because the same shift affected all workers.

Thus, by 1940 the occupational advancement that could be expected for Negroes from more than thirty years of service in the meat industry had not taken place. No significant entry into white collar employment had occurred, but an even harsher fact is that there had been no gains in skilled manual employment— foreman and craft positions. Apparently, very few of the many Negro production workers who had first entered the industry between World War I and 1940 were promoted to foreman positions or were selected for skilled production jobs. The only significant change in the occupational distribution of Negroes by 1940 was a shift from unskilled to semiskilled jobs; this was brought about by technological progress in the industry and did not represent any relative improvement for Negroes. The one possible gain made by black workers, as suggested by Herbst, was an enlargement during World War I of their employment as semiskilled butchers; this job was among the better of the operative positions available in the meat industry.[121] However, there is no way of assessing the extent of this advancement, or even of being certain that it did take place.[122]

The 1960's

Purcell states that Negroes made substantial occupational gains in the 1950's in the Chicago Swift plant which he studied.[123] It is likely that similar progress was made in other plants in those years, and that it had its beginning in the 1940's. The demand for skilled labor during World War II was much in

---

[121] Herbst, *op. cit.*, p. xxii.

[122] Survey in 1937 of about 45 percent of meat packing employment conducted by the U.S. Department of Labor found a much better occupational status of Negroes than did either the 1930 or 1940 census of population. This survey, covering only manual workers, found that 20 percent of the Negro males were in skilled jobs, 47 percent in semiskilled and 33 percent in unskilled jobs. The comparative figures for all males were 24 percent skilled, 48 percent semiskilled, and 28 percent unskilled. There were many differences in scope between this Department of Labor survey and the censuses of population. However, such large discrepancies between the survey and the censuses in the skill distribution of Negro employees could be due only to differences in skill classifications which were used or to inaccuracies produced by the Department of Labor survey (because the census of population data are consistent for 1930 and 1940). On the former point, the survey may have classified certain butchering jobs as skilled, while the census of population classified them as semiskilled (operatives). The survey results are in the *Monthly Labor Review*, under the title, "Earnings and Hours in the Meat Packing Industry, December 1937," Vol. 39 (October 1939), pp. 936-959.

[123] Theodore V. Purcell, *Blue Collar Man* (Cambridge: Harvard University Press, 1960), p. 127. It should be noted that the census did not give meat industry occupational breakdowns in 1950 and 1960.

excess of available supply, and it is likely that during the war some blacks as well as whites were upgraded into skilled employment in the meat industry. The first two Executive Orders pertaining to fair employment practices were issued during World War II, and they may have had an impact on firms which were supplying large amounts of meat to the federal government. It was in the 1940's, also, that unionization of the meat industry became firmly established. The UPWA probably had an almost immediate impact on the job status of Negroes because of its active antidiscrimination orientation.

Our field survey provides data about the present occupational status of Negroes in the meat industry. It should be remembered, however, that these data are not perfectly comparable with the information obtained from the censuses of population: only about one-half of the meat industry is covered, the sample is biased toward large firms, and the information is obtained from employers rather than from individuals. Also pertinent here is the possibility that some employees may have misclassified themselves under the census or may have been misclassified into the various occupational categories used by employers. Nevertheless, our data do provide occupational measures which are at least roughly comparable to those provided by the censuses of population for earlier years. The broad occupational distributions for 1966 are shown in Table 27.

It can be seen from the table that Negroes have still not made any progress in increasing the nonmanual percentage of their employment: it was close to one percent of total Negro

TABLE 27. *Meat Industry*

Total and Negro Employment by Occupation

1966

Occupation	Total		Negro		Negro Percent of Total Employment
	Number	Percent	Number	Percent	
Nonmanual	34,180	23.0	260	1.2	0.8
Craftsmen	18,880	12.7	2,400	11.2	12.7
Unskilled and semiskilled	95,540	64.3	18,770	87.6	19.6
All occupations	148,600	100.0	21,430	100.0	14.4

Source: Data in the author's possession.

employment in 1966, as it was more than fifty years ago. There
have been substantial increases, however, in the employment
of black workers in skilled manual positions—11.2 percent held
craft and foreman jobs in 1966 as compared with only 1.3 percent in 1940.[124] There is no way of determining from our data
the number of black workers who are foremen, as opposed to
craftsmen, but interviews with officials and workers in the industry suggested that it is comparatively small.

Another way of showing the present occupational status of
Negro workers relative to their earlier status is to compare the
shares of nonmanual and skilled employment held by Negroes
in 1940 and 1966 (Tables 25 and 27). In 1940, Negroes comprised less than 0.5 percent of all nonmanual employment in the
meat industry, while in 1966 the comparable figure was 0.8
percent. Black workers held about one percent of the skilled
manual jobs in 1940 and about 13 percent of these jobs in 1966.
These comparisons of Negro representation disclose the same results as the comparisons of occupational distribution; no gains
have been made in the nonmanual occupations, but there has
been substantial movement into craft and foreman positions.

Have Negroes in the meat industry now obtained equal access
to skilled manual jobs? The data in Table 27 suggest that
equality has almost been achieved because the percentage of
black workers who hold craft and foreman jobs is nearly as
large as that of white workers in these jobs. The figures are
misleading in this respect, however, because they combine two
quite different occupational sectors—nonmanual and manual. The
question of equal access to skilled manual jobs should consider
the skill distributions of manual workers only. Nonmanual
workers comprise a quite separate occupational group in terms
of skills and interests; most have been hired directly into white
collar positions from external (to the firm) labor markets and
are either not qualified for or not interested in manual employment. Combining nonmanual workers with other employees
lowers the percentage of whites in the skilled manual classification, thus giving a different picture of the skill distribution than
is obtained by excluding nonmanual workers.

Considering the manual group only (this group is roughly
equivalent to the unionized sector of the work force, plus fore-

---

[124] It is possible that part of this increase is due to changes in classifications—classifying skilled butchers as craftsmen in 1966 and as operatives
in 1940 (by the census of population).

men), 11.2 percent of the Negroes in the meat industry were in skilled jobs in 1966, with the remainder in low-skilled positions; by comparison, 16.5 percent of the white manual workers held skilled jobs. Thus, black workers have some way to go before they are employed as frequently in craft and foreman jobs as are whites.

Although there is underrepresentation of Negroes in skilled manual jobs, it is very minor compared to that in nonmanual employment. It is a fact that Negroes have never held more than a token number of white collar positions in the meat industry.

Very recent occupational data for the largest firms in the meat industry (covering their meat and other operations) disclose more precisely the very poor position of Negroes in white collar employment (Table 28). At the beginning of 1968, approximately 200 of 24,000 white collar positions in the four largest firms—Swift, Armour, Wilson, and Morrell—were filled

TABLE 28. *Meat Industry*

Total and Negro Employment by Occupation
Four Largest Firms, 1968

Occupation	Total		Negro		Negro Percent of Total Employment
	Number	Percent	Number	Percent	
Officials and managers	7,872	9.1	24	0.2	0.3
Professionals	1,839	2.1	10	0.1	0.5
Technicians	888	1.0	17	0.2	1.9
Sales workers	6,071	7.1	26	0.2	0.4
Office and clerical	7,726	9.0	130	1.2	1.7
Total white collar	24,396	28.3	207	1.9	0.8
Craftsmen	8,875	10.3	1,123	10.7	12.7
Operatives	34,240	39.7	5,427	51.6	15.8
Laborers	17,152	19.9	3,401	32.4	19.8
Service workers	1,547	1.8	355	3.4	22.9
Total blue collar	61,814	71.7	10,306	98.1	16.7
Total	86,210	100.0	10,513	100.0	

Source: Data in the author's possession.

by Negroes. Blacks comprised only 0.8 percent of white collar employment in these firms, compared to their share of 16.7 percent of blue collar employment. Most Negroes in white collar employment in these four firms held clerical jobs; very few were in sales, managerial, or professional positions.

The only favorable comment that can be made about Negro white collar employment in the meat industry is that it is increasing. This is shown in Tables 29-31 with data for 205 meat establishments in 1964 and for 252 establishments in 1966 and 1968. (Similar data for four regions of the United States are presented in Appendix Tables A-6-A-17.) Between 1964 and 1968, the share of white collar jobs held by Negroes rose from 0.5 to 1.6 percent. Between 1966 and 1968, the number of Negroes employed in white collar positions increased from 185 to over 400. The number of Negroes in four of five nonmanual categories rose substantially, but declined by more than one-half in the professional category (the latter change may reflect reclassifications of some employees). Thus, the meat industry is apparently attempting to increase its utilization of blacks in nonmanual jobs. With blacks holding only 100 of 8,400 managerial jobs and 24 of 4,800 sales positions, a great amount of room for improvement does exist.

Industrial personnel managers gave three reasons for the relative absence of Negroes from white collar occupations: (1) because of declining employment in the industry, the average age of white collar employees is high, turnover is low, and white collar job opportunities available to Negroes are few; (2) many nonmanual workers in the meat industry obtained their jobs through promotion from manual employment and few black manual workers seek promotion to nonmanual positions; (3) few qualified Negroes are available for the nonmanual positions which are filled from external labor markets.

There is undoubtedly some validity to the first explanation, but the extent to which it accounts for the low employment of blacks in the white collar sector is unknown. The explanation has less relevance to clerical jobs than to the higher status nonmanual jobs because employee turnover in the former is less sensitive to declining industry employment.

Nor is it possible to fully assess the second explanation. One would need to know, first of all, the number of white collar employees in the industry who have been promoted from manual work. It would be surprising to find that, except for foremen,

TABLE 29. *Meat Industry*

Employment by Race, Sex, and Occupational Group

205 Establishments, 1964

Occupation	All Employees			Male			Female		
	Total	Negro	Percent Negro	Total	Negro	Percent Negro	Total	Negro	Percent Negro
Officials and managers	7,296	25	0.3	7,254	25	0.3	42	0	0.0
Professionals	2,217	18	0.8	2,133	16	0.8	84	2	2.4
Technicians	910	11	1.2	785	9	1.1	125	2	1.6
Sales workers	4,899	7	0.1	4,801	7	0.1	98	0	0.0
Office and clerical	8,425	60	0.7	4,089	33	0.8	4,336	27	0.6
Total white collar	23,747	121	0.5	19,062	90	0.5	4,685	31	0.7
Craftsmen	13,890	1,781	12.8	13,496	1,739	12.9	394	42	10.7
Operatives	40,800	6,209	15.2	33,387	5,608	16.8	7,413	601	8.1
Laborers	24,202	5,315	22.0	15,600	3,583	23.0	8,602	1,732	20.1
Service workers	2,384	454	19.0	2,073	432	20.8	311	22	7.1
Total blue collar	81,276	13,759	16.9	64,556	11,362	17.6	16,720	2,397	14.3
Total	105,023	13,880	13.2	83,618	11,452	13.7	21,405	2,428	11.3

Source: Data in the author's possession.

Note: Further breakdown by regions can be found in Appendix Tables A-6—A-9.

TABLE 30. *Meat Industry*

Employment by Race, Sex, and Occupational Group
252 Establishments, 1966

Occupation	All Employees			Male			Female		
	Total	Negro	Percent Negro	Total	Negro	Percent Negro	Total	Negro	Percent Negro
Officials and managers	7,966	39	0.5	7,912	38	0.5	54	1	1.9
Professionals	1,824	24	1.3	1,755	24	1.4	69	0	0.0
Technicians	1,090	12	1.1	941	11	1.2	149	1	0.7
Sales workers	5,308	13	0.2	5,202	13	0.2	106	0	0.0
Office and clerical	8,860	97	1.1	4,233	59	1.4	4,627	38	0.8
Total white collar	25,048	185	0.7	20,043	145	0.7	5,005	40	0.8
Craftsmen	14,548	1,692	11.6	14,237	1,684	11.8	311	8	2.6
Operatives	41,440	6,530	15.8	34,748	5,710	16.4	6,692	820	12.3
Laborers	27,179	5,972	22.0	17,319	3,895	22.5	9,860	2,077	21.1
Service workers	2,619	546	20.8	2,344	515	22.0	275	31	11.3
Total blue collar	85,786	14,740	17.2	68,648	11,804	17.2	17,138	2,936	17.1
Total	110,834	14,925	13.5	88,691	11,949	13.5	22,143	2,976	13.4

Source: Data in the author's possession.

Note: Further breakdown by regions can be found in Appendix Tables A-10—A-13.

TABLE 31. *Meat Industry*
Employment by Race, Sex, and Occupational Group
252 Establishments, 1968

Occupation	All Employees			Male			Female		
	Total	Negro	Percent Negro	Total	Negro	Percent Negro	Total	Negro	Percent Negro
Officials and managers	8,445	98	1.2	8,378	96	1.1	67	2	3.0
Professionals	1,902	11	0.5	1,792	10	0.6	110	1	0.9
Technicians	1,110	35	3.2	986	32	3.2	124	3	2.4
Sales workers	4,809	24	0.5	4,710	23	0.5	99	1	1.0
Office and clerical	8,576	239	2.8	3,747	91	2.4	4,829	148	3.1
Total white collar	24,842	407	1.6	19,613	252	1.3	5,229	155	3.0
Craftsmen	14,294	1,715	12.0	14,063	1,682	12.0	231	33	14.3
Operatives	45,246	7,789	17.2	37,006	6,535	17.7	8,240	1,254	15.2
Laborers	26,752	5,993	22.4	16,917	3,707	21.9	9,835	2,286	23.2
Service workers	2,165	452	20.9	1,953	427	21.9	212	25	11.8
Total blue collar	88,457	15,949	18.0	69,939	12,351	17.7	18,518	3,598	19.4
Total	113,299	16,356	14.4	89,552	12,603	14.1	23,747	3,753	15.8

Source: Data in the author's possession.

Note: Further breakdown by regions can be found in Appendix Tables A-14 —A-17.

many of the industry's clerical, sales, professional, and managerial employees are former production workers; as mentioned earlier, firms usually hire these kinds of employees from external labor markets. Also, earnings are much greater in manual jobs than in most clerical positions and this, too, restricts movement from production to office jobs. The second point one would want to investigate in order to assess the internal promotion factor is the comparative propensity of black and white workers to apply for promotions to nonmanual positions, and, if blacks do apply less frequently, why this is so. Intuitively, it seems unlikely that the internal promotion explanation accounts for much of the low white collar representation of Negroes in the meat industry.

The third explanation, that few qualified Negroes are available for white collar employment, undoubtedly has some validity; this comment is heard repeatedly from employers who are trying to increase their employment of Negroes. Granted this fact, how does Negro white collar employment in the meat industry compare with that in other industries? A full answer to that question will be found in the final sectors of the general project of which this study is a part. A partial answer, however, can now be given by focusing on the Chicago metropolitan area.

In 1965 the three largest meat packing firms—Swift, Armour, and Wilson—had their headquarters in downtown Chicago. (Morrell had its headquarters divided between Chicago and Ottumwa, Iowa in 1965.) At that time, black workers represented almost 14 percent of employed persons in the Chicago metropolitan area.[125] A large proportion of Negro workers had relatively easy transportation access to the offices of the packing firms because most lived in Chicago's inner city; however, few Negroes held jobs in these offices. The three firms had only 22 black workers among the 3,300 white collar employees in their general offices in January 1965 (a minor percentage of these employees performed work relating to industries other than meat products); two of the headquarters offices were almost lily-white—one employed three female Negro clerks and the other had two black clerks, one male and one female.[126]

---

[125] Equal Employment Opportunity Commission, Information Release, Washington, August 6, 1967.

[126] Data in the author's possession.

Three years later, in January 1968, the three firms had increased their white collar employment of Negroes to 62, or 1.8 percent of the total.[127] By way of contrast, Negro representation in white collar employment in all Chicago firms was 4.7 percent in early 1966.[128] Thus, despite marked gains, the employment of Negroes in the headquarters offices of the three largest meat packing firms remains well below the Negro share of all white collar employment in Chicago. Therefore, the unavailability of qualified Negro employees does not appear to be the major influence behind the low representation of Negroes in the Chicago meat packing offices.

Occupational Change Summary

We can quickly summarize the long-term occupational status of Negroes in the meat industry. Between 1910 and 1940 there was little change. Between 1940 and the present, Negro employment in skilled manual jobs rose sharply, and equality of representation in these jobs is likely to be achieved soon. No significant long-run improvements have occurred in the white collar employment of Negroes. In the last few years, the larger firms in the industry have increased the number of Negroes in white collar positions, but even so, 98 percent of all black workers in the meat industry hold manual jobs at the present time.

---

[127] *Ibid.*

[128] Equal Employment Opportunity Commission, *loc. cit.*

CHAPTER VI.

Job Performance and Discrimination

It is much easier and less time-consuming to count people than to study or closely observe them. Although information on numbers of Negroes employed in American industries is generally available, little is known about their comparative performance and treatment. Fortunately, there are three studies which together provide a small amount of information on Negro performance in the meat industry. The first of these is Alma Herbst's already noted research in Chicago in the 1920's. Although she interviewed company officials in twenty-four meat packing firms, her data on job turnover are confined to one medium-sized establishment. The second is a self-survey of the UPWA conducted in 1949 [129] in two parts: a survey of UPWA local union officers, and interviews with white and black workers in three meat packing centers—Fort Worth, Kansas City, and Omaha. Thus, this study provides information concerning attitudes and opinions of local union officers and members. The study was directed and carried out by academicians, but was sponsored by the UPWA International Executive Board. The reader should recognize that, under these circumstances, local union officials and members may not have been entirely candid in their responses.

Finally, Father Theodore Purcell's research at three large Swift facilities in the early 1950's provides much relevant information. The approximate racial composition of the work forces at the three plants was as follows: Chicago, 1,900 whites and 2,100 Negroes; East St. Louis, 1,100 whites and 900 Negroes; Kansas City, 1,200 whites, including 200 Mexican-Americans, and 800 Negroes. Purcell's research should not be considered as pertinent only to Swift and Company; it is likely that his findings in the three Swift plants applied generally to large metropolitan plants in the meat industry in the 1950's.

---

[129] John Hope II, *op. cit.*

Perhaps the major weakness of all three studies is that they frequently present racial data without controlling for the influence of nonracial variables. The data must therefore be viewed with considerable caution.

More current information on Negro job performance and on discrimination is provided by the author's interviews with company officials, national and local union officers, and Negro and Mexican workers. These interviews took place in the summer of 1968 in the Chicago headquarters of the major meat packing firms and unions, and in seven midwestern cities in which large meat packing plants are located.

PERFORMANCE

Historically, the black worker in the meat industry has been labeled an "unsteady" employee, one who is frequently absent from work and is likely to quit his job more readily than other workers. It is likely, however, that most, or all, of this unsteadiness was related to the nature of the jobs held by Negroes in the industry.

Job Turnover and Absenteeism

John R. Commons, writing in 1904 about Negroes in Chicago meat packing, stated that they did not advance to skilled positions because "they dislike the long apprenticeship and steady work at low pay which lead to such positions," and "they are not steady workers at the low wages of the Slav." [130] The evidence for these conclusions is not given.

In one medium-sized plant studied by Herbst, records for the years 1922 to 1926 showed that Negroes were discharged and laid off more frequently than whites, but that they quit less often. These records, however, did not indicate the job levels at which blacks and whites were employed. After considering job levels, Herbst decided that the comparative job turnover of Negro workers could not be determined. [131]

Perhaps more significant was the fact that in the Chicago yards "employers unanimously complain of his [the Negro's] unsteadiness, of the rapid rate at which he passes through establishments in the Yards, of his casualness in 'throwing up a

---

[130] John R. Commons, *loc cit.*, p. 30.

[131] Herbst, *op. cit.*, pp. 139, 147.

job.' " [132] Personnel officials in the firms studied by Herbst were of the opinion that "the unskilled Negro laborers who perform the disagreeable work and the women [especially Negro women] are the nucleus of the concentrated phenomenon of turnover." [133]

Much, perhaps all, of the high job turnover of black workers which existed in Chicago meat packing (we have no evidence pertaining to other industry locations) through the 1920's and perhaps into World War II can be ascribed to their frequent employment on jobs which were disagreeable in terms of working conditions or were temporary—existing only during peak production periods. In addition, there is no doubt that some Negroes who had recently migrated from the rural South found it difficult to adjust to the rigid time requirements of factory work. Problems of adapting work forces to factory schedules and discipline have pervaded the process of industrialization wherever it has occurred, and they must also have accompanied the employment in northern factories of Negroes with rural backgrounds. Unfortunately, it is unlikely that many evaluations by employees of Negro job qualifications took into account these nonracial influences on turnover. Instead, the high, visible turnover of black workers which characterized Chicago meat packing through World War I was accepted then and for many years to come as evidence that Negroes were less likely than whites to be steady, long service workers.

Purcell compiled some data on turnover in the early 1950's for the three Swift plants which he studied. These data are not broken down on a racial basis; however, the Chicago plant, which had the largest proportion of black employees, had a quit rate less than one-half of the rates in the other two plants.[134]

Purcell also collected statistics on absenteeism, and on this measure of job performance the record of Negroes was inferior to that of whites. His data are set forth in Table 32.

These data are not standardized for job level or for other factors. (Purcell did present absentee figures for several length-of-service categories; they show results generally similar to those presented in Table 32.) The tendency of Negroes to work fewer weeks each year than whites may have been due to their more frequent employment in undesirable jobs, age differences between black and white workers, or other factors unrelated to race.

---

[132] *Ibid*, p. 127.

[133] *Ibid*, p. 72.

[134] Purcell, *Blue Collar Man, op. cit.*, p. 52.

TABLE 32. *Meat Industry*
Percentage of Employees Working Less than 52 Weeks
Selected Cities, by Race and Sex
1950 and 1952

Region	Male		Female	
	White	Negro	White	Negro
Chicago (1950)	19%	26%	28%	63%
Kansas City (1952)	14	27	7	29
East St. Louis (1952)	5	11	1	—

Source: Theodore H. Purcell, *Blue Collar Man* (Cambridge: Harvard University Press, 1960), p. 53.

The 1949 survey of UPWA members showed that voluntary absence from work was about the same for white and black respondents in Omaha and Fort Worth. Layoffs from work occurred at similar rates for the two groups in Omaha, but in Fort Worth a much larger percentage of blacks was laid off for at least one day during the year. Average length of job tenure was greater for Negroes than for whites in Omaha, but the reverse was true in Fort Worth.[135] In general, these findings were supported by the UPWA survey of local union officers; the number of respondents who thought that Negroes had better records than whites on turnover and tardiness was roughly equal to the number who believed Negroes to be inferior on these matters. The evaluation of absenteeism was an exception to the general results. On this job performance criterion, 29 percent of the local union respondents thought that Negroes were less satisfactory than whites, 15 percent said that Negroes were more satisfactory, and 56 percent indicated no difference.[136]

Wage Garnishments

Purcell collected data in two plants on the assignment of workers' wages for failure to pay debts. In Chicago, he found a rate of 120 assignments per week for a work force of 4,000; in East St. Louis, where about one-half as many workers were employed, the rate was 19 a week. In both places almost all garnishments were against Negro workers.[137]

---

[135] Hope, *op. cit.*, pp. 36, 144.

[136] *Ibid.*, p. 32.

[137] Purcell, *Blue Collar Man, op. cit.*, p. 54.

Over-all Performance

Purcell asked white foremen in the three Swift plants to compare total job performance of their white and black workers.
The results were unfavorable to the latter. Thirty-three percent
of the foremen in Kansas City, 53 percent in East St. Louis, and
77 percent in Chicago preferred white workers; 9 percent, 5 percent, and 4 percent, respectively, preferred black workers. The
remainder of those who had expressed an opinion stated no
preference.[138] It is impossible to determine the extent to which
the views expressed by the foremen respondents reflected their
general racial views rather than their direct experience with
workers. In addition, as indicated earlier, there was a good deal
of white resentment against the Negro leadership of the Swift
local in Chicago, and these feelings probably had an impact on
the Negro-white worker comparisons made by the Chicago foremen. UPWA local officers, in contrast to the foremen questioned
by Purcell, gave very similar ratings of job performance to
black and white workers.[139]

Current Performance

The author's study was not designed to provide the kind of
data on job performance which were obtained in the intensive
investigations of Purcell or by the questionnaire method of the
UPWA self-survey. This proved to be fortunate because company officials interviewed indicated that most of these data do
not exist in their firms, and if they did exist, their sensitive nature would preclude their use.

In these interviews, every question directed to the comparative
job performance of black and white workers but one was an-
swered by an indication of no difference between the groups.
The one exception was a statement by a personnel officer of a
major firm that the incidence of wage attachments was substantially greater among blacks than among whites.

The information presented here is not sufficient in quantity or
direction to warrant conclusions about the comparative performance of black workers in the meat industry. In other
words, there is no reliable evidence that Negroes perform any

---

[138] *Ibid.*, p. 93. These figures were calculated by excluding those foremen
who gave no clear comparative comment—4 percent in Chicago, 31 percent
in Kansas City, and none in East St. Louis.

[139] Hope, *op. cit.*, p. 32.

less capably than other workers in the industry. Wage garnishments are apparently much more common among blacks than among whites; however, garnishments do not necessarily affect job performance.

DISCRIMINATION

Historically, the following kinds of discrimination have been alleged against the meat industry: (1) failure to give minority persons equal opportunity for advancement to skilled maintenance, foreman, and white collar jobs; (2) exclusion of Negroes from certain production departments; (3) refusal to employ Negro women; and (4) requiring black workers to use segregated plant facilities.

Job Advancement

Many of the most desirable blue collar jobs in meat packing plants are in what the industry calls the "mechanical department." This department is chiefly concerned with maintenance of plant and equipment and, therefore, employs many skilled craft workers such as carpenters, machinists, and electricians. The jobs are attractive because wage rates are higher and working conditions better than on most production jobs.

It is clear from the census statistics quoted in the previous chapter that few Negroes were employed in the skilled jobs of the mechanical department or in foreman positions before 1940. It cannot be determined whether they were blocked from these jobs because of discrimination; data on worker qualifications are not available. It is hardly plausible, however, that in 1940, after black workers had been employed in the industry for over 30 years, only one percent of them was qualified to work in skilled craft and foreman jobs.

As discussed in the previous chapter, it is likely that craft and foreman jobs became increasingly available to black workers after the beginning of World War II. Purcell's investigations clearly show, however, that Negroes continued to be very much underrepresented in craft, foreman, and white collar occupations even in the 1950's. In the East St. Louis Swift plant, with almost 1,000 Negro employees in 1954, there were no blacks in office work, sales, or plant supervision, and black men worked "hardly at all" in the mechanical department. In the Kansas City Swift plant, with 800 Negroes in 1953, one was an assistant foreman, none worked in office or sales jobs, and very few were in the skilled craft jobs. Only in the Chicago Swift plant, where they were a majority in the UPWA bargaining unit, had Negroes made substantial advances into these attractive jobs.[140]

Though objective conclusions about discrimination in job advancement cannot be given, subjective evaluations of minority persons on this matter can be cited from previous studies. In the East St. Louis and Kansas City Swift plants in the 1950's (no data are available for the Chicago plant), more than 70 percent of the black workers thought that they did not have opportunities for job advancement that were equal to those of white workers; 31 percent of Mexican workers, almost all of whom were employed at Kansas City, thought that this kind of discrimination existed against members of their ethnic group.[141] The 1950 UPWA survey produced similar findings. One-half of all local union officers who responded thought that there was some discrimination against Negroes in job advancement within the bargaining unit. A majority of the black workers interviewed also believed that advancement discrimination existed.[142] Thus, in the 1950's, Negro perceptions of their opportunities for job advancement were congruent with their actual underrepresentation in attractive jobs.

In the previous chapter it was shown that 11 percent of all Negro manual workers in 1966 were in craft and foreman jobs compared with 16 percent of white employees. These figures indicate substantial movement of Negroes into craft jobs in mechanical departments and, to a lesser extent, foreman positions over the last twenty-five years. There may or may not have been continual progress since World War II, but the author's field interviews indicated that important progress had definitely occurred during the 1960's, especially in the last few years under the impetus of civil rights laws and agitation, and the growth of public policies against discrimination. Most union officials and minority group persons alike stated that Negroes and Mexicans have been more frequently selected for skilled craft positions in the last few years than previously. In some instances, tests have been eliminated or reduced in importance for selection to mechanical department apprenticeships, sometimes because of

---

[140] Purcell, *Blue Collar Man, op. cit.*, pp. 127-128.

[141] *Ibid.*, pp. 135, 270.

[142] Hope, *op. cit.*, pp. 36, 45.

union pressure, and at other times through company decisions taken independently. At present, most mechanical department jobs in the industry are awarded on the basis of seniority.

It should be noted that, although locals of the UPWA and the Amalgamated have been a positive force in seeking equal access to all blue collar jobs, union *members* have not always supported their leadership on these matters. The author was told of various forms of harassment which minority employees have encountered while employed in "helper" or apprentice positions among skilled craftsmen. Also, management in some plants retains discriminatory selection procedures for skilled positions only because of the tacit approval of white workers. In these instances, the white workers have not been influenced by their union's antidiscrimination policies and educational programs.

All company and most union officials interviewed stated that Negroes and Mexicans now have opportunities equal to those of others for obtaining jobs in the mechanical department. Not all Negroes and Mexicans agree, however; approximately one-half of those interviewed indicated that they do not receive equal consideration for these jobs or that the tests used in selecting employees for the mechanical departments discriminate against them because of their minority cultural background.

The belief that discrimination exists in the selection of foremen is widespread among the minority employees interviewed. Whether this belief is justified, is not known. The evidence used by minority persons to support it is the low representation of Negroes and Mexicans among foremen; by itself this is not sufficient evidence. Currently, a salary incentive problem complicates the question of discrimination in foreman selection. Many production workers, both black and white, will not accept promotions to foreman positions because they feel that salaries do not adequately compensate for the additional responsibilities entailed in the job.[143] One Mexican worker who alleged that minority persons did not receive fair treatment in foreman selection stated in the same breath that in the last few years he had turned down three offers of foreman positions because the company "wouldn't meet my price." All of the company spokesmen indicated that they are trying to increase the numbers of Negroes and Mexicans who are foremen, and that they are having

---

[143] In an effort to meet this problem, Armour has now begun to pay its foremen time and one-half after 40 hours in a week, instead of after 48, which was its past practice.

trouble finding minority persons who are both qualified and interested. Some of these officials seemed to believe that minority workers are less interested than other employees in taking foreman jobs, though this was never said explicitly.

The current low employment of Negroes in white collar occupations has already been discussed. If these low figures are a result of discrimination, the discrimination may occur in promotion or in hiring. It has already been suggested, however, that in the meat industry, as in other industries, most white collar employees are hired directly into their jobs from outside the firms. Thus, discrimination in hiring, rather than in promotion from manual work, is more relevant to the Negroes' white collar status.

Although one can never be certain about the absence of discrimination, it is this author's belief that, with the exception of sales positions, the major meat firms do not at present discriminate in the hiring of minority persons for white collar positions or in their advancement to the better white collar jobs. The meat industry, like many others, is now trying to rectify past omissions—omissions which are evident from the data of the previous chapter—and, if anything, is discriminating in favor of employing the promising black worker and advancing him to positions of increasing pay and status. These statements do not hold for the sales occupation, however. Several company officials were quite candid about this. They (or more accurately, operating officials of their firms) fear loss of customers if black persons are given sales positions. This view remains a hypothesis rather than a fact, because it has so seldom been tested. Even if white consumers do object to black salesmen, black people eat meat too, and certainly there are some sales locations in which the employment of black sales personnel would be well received by consumers.

There does not appear to be any discrimination in the large meat firms in advancing Negroes to skilled butchering jobs. Some black workers think that they are underrepresented in these jobs relative to their total employment, but if this is true it is more a result of departmental exclusion than of discrimination in advancement. In the unionized part of the meat industry, once a worker is employed in a department he can advance to more skilled jobs within the department according to his seniority rank.

Departmental Exclusion

Negroes were excluded from certain departments of meat pack- ing firms until after World War II in most plants, and until the mid-1950's in some. This was in addition to exclusion of black workers from the mechanical and white collar departments where discrimination was fundamentally occupational—to keep Negroes out of certain jobs—rather than departmental. Departments practicing exclusion usually were those in which final processing and packaging functions were performed, for example, the bacon, oleo, and cheese departments. The basis for discrimination was that the meat packing firms did not want the consuming public to believe "black hands" might have touched the final meat prod- ucts. Anomalies developed from the implementation of this pol- icy, however. In one firm, Herbst found that no Negro women were employed in oleo packaging, even though the packing itself was done entirely by machine, because visitors frequently came through the work room.[144] The same firm used Negro men to pack oleo into pails because that process was never seen by the public. This kind of practice continued at least into the 1940's. In 1941, the PWOC local at a Chicago Wilson plant protested because black workers were taken out of packaging lines when visitors were brought through the plant.[145] In 1949, 60 percent of the UPWA locals indicated that Negroes were being excluded from one or more departments, most frequently the mechanical department, "as a matter of custom." [146]

The author's interviews and Purcell's prior research suggest that Negroes in most plants had attained at least nominal entry to all departments except the mechanical department by the mid-1950's. Nevertheless, very uneven departmental distribu- tions of black employees continued to exist into the 1960's in some locations. Negroes were usually found in large numbers in the dressing departments where the livestock are killed and their carcases prepared for further butchering, and they were infrequently employed in the boning departments where many skilled cutting operations are performed.[147] Working conditions are considered to be more disagreeable in the dressing or "kill"

---

[144] Herbst, *op. cit.*, p. 80.

[145] Kampfert, *loc. cit.*, Part IV.

[146] Hope, *op. cit.*, p. 27.

[147] Purcell, *Blue Collar Man, op. cit.*, pp. 127-128.

departments, as they are frequently called, than in the boning departments.

A few of the minority persons interviewed by the author in the summer of 1968 felt that some departments still discriminate against them. Most minority workers, however, believed that all departments, with the possible exception of the mechanical department, were open to them. Even so, black workers tend to be somewhat concentrated in the kill departments and under-represented in the more desirable boning operations.[148]

The nature of seniority in the industry contributes to these departmental differences. In most unionized meat packing firms, workers establish job bidding rights, based on seniority, in only one department. Thus, if a worker has ten years of seniority in a department, he is reluctant to transfer to another where he would have no seniority and would have to take the least desirable job. The initial employment of many Negroes in the industry is in one of the kill departments, either because whites will not take these jobs or, some persons allege, because plant managers think of these jobs as "Negro work." Given the departmental seniority system, many blacks never leave the kill departments.

Negro workers employed in several different meat packing plants told the author of devious means which, they alleged, are often used to keep blacks out of the desirable departments. They claimed that in some departments new Negro workers are consistently terminated from employment before they have completed the probationary period (often thirty days, though it varies among plants) required by union contract for the attainment of seniority in the department. In contrast, white workers who are hired on a temporary basis not to exceed the probationary period may be carried beyond it, enabling them to establish departmental seniority. Where minority persons and union spokesmen agreed that there was no departmental discrimination, it was frequently stated that this condition had been achieved only within the last few years.

Departmental discrimination was found in a careful study of a large plant in Omaha in 1962.[149] The researcher found that initial employment of Negroes in the less desirable departments

---

[148] Interviews with various industry officials, summer 1968.

[149] John A. Ballweg, "A Study of Inter-Department Mobility of Workers in Meat Packing Plant: Volitional Versus Non-Volitional," Master's thesis, Department of Sociology, University of Omaha, 1962.

was much more frequent than was the case for whites, and that Negroes less often transferred to the more attractive departments than did whites.

Apparently there remains some discrimination in the meat industry which results in limiting Negro access to the most desirable production departments, but the author's investigations found that this kind of discrimination is much less widespread now than in the past, and it probably does not exist at all in a majority of the larger plants. However, even if such discrimination is nonexistent at present, the effects of its having been practiced in the past could be a potential problem in the industry's race relations. In a number of industries, past discriminatory hiring practices combined with a departmental seniority system have led to demands on the part of Negro employees that they be granted special opportunities to transfer to better jobs in other departments in order to compensate them for such past practices. In the paper and tobacco industries, where discrimination was much more widespread and longer adhered to than in the meat industry, these claims have been supported by the courts.[150]

The potential legal problems which the meat industry may have to face because of its departmental seniority system are much less serious than those encountered in the aforementioned industries. As previously noted, hiring practices and the departmental seniority system have produced a somewhat more favorable departmental distribution for whites than for blacks, but the differences are such that they can be remedied by the transfer of a relatively small number of workers, and the evidence indicates that movement toward a fully equitable distribution of Negro workers is taking place.

It is actually the reduction of plant operations which causes the greatest difficulties for the seniority system in the meat industry, and, on this matter, white as well as black workers are affected. As the work force in an aging plant is reduced, workers from the closed departments can move into other departments only at the bottom of the departmental seniority rosters. This means that the workers affected by plant reduc-

---

[150] *Quarles* v. *Philip Morris, Inc.*, 279 F.Supp. 505 (E.D. Va., 1968), involving the tobacco industry; and *United States* v. *Local 189, United Papermakers and Paperworkers, et al.*, 282 F. Supp. 39 (E.D. La., 1968), affirmed, U.S. Court of Appeals, Fifth Circuit, June 29, 1969, involving the paper industry. Seniority systems in both these industries are examined in other studies in the Racial Policies of American Industry series.

tions must accept less desirable jobs as well as insecurity of employment if they wish to retain their plant employment. These seniority matters could become racial issues where plant reductions disproportionately affect Negro workers, but it is more likely that they will be widely recognized for what they are— complex problems concerning the equitable distribution of a reduced number of jobs among an existing work force.

Prior to the merger of the UPWA and the Amalgamated, officials of the former were considering various ways to revise the departmental seniority system so as to provide more protection for older workers. Since both employers and employees often prefer departmental to wider seniority because it causes less dislocation during employment changes, strong opposition to changing the system is likely. If proposals to revise the seniority system are put forward, workers are likely to divide on age or some other dimension, rather than along racial lines.

Negro Women

The meat industry has at various times in its history discriminated against hiring Negro women. A UPWA official, active in union organizing in Chicago meat packing for a quarter of a century, wrote that the Chicago Swift plants had not hired any black women between 1909 and 1937, and only began to employ a few after the PWOC demanded that they do so.[151] This statement exaggerates the intensity of exclusion of Negro women— some were hired by Swift in this period—but it is correct in its implication of severe discrimination. Purcell found that the Swift plants in East St. Louis and Kansas City had stopped hiring black women in the 1920's and 1930's respectively.[152] More generally, between 1930 and 1940 the Negro percent of female employment in the industry fell from 6.7 to 2.5 (Appendix Table A-1). Only 800 of the 31,700 females employed in the industry in 1940 were Negro.

This type of discrimination lessened after the beginning of World War II; 11.3 percent and 12.8 percent of female employment was held by Negroes in 1950 and 1960 respectively. It was by no means completely eliminated, however. Purcell's investigations revealed that although the Kansas City Swift plant began hiring Negro women during World War II, they comprised

---

[151] Kampfert, *loc. cit.*, Part II, p. 6.

[152] Purcell, *Blue Collar Man, op. cit.*, p. 127.

only one percent of his randomly drawn sample of workers in that plant in 1953.[153] No Negro women were employed in the East St. Louis Swift plant when Purcell ended his study there in 1957,[154] and even in 1965, when a majority of the East St. Louis population was black, none of the 250 women employed in the Swift plant were black.[155] The arbitration award in 1951, which found that Swift had discriminated against the employment of Negro women in one of its Chicago plants, has already been mentioned.

In 1968, Negroes comprised 12 percent of all female manual workers in the industry's eight largest firms;[156] thus there is probably little, if any, discrimination at present in the hiring of black women for manual jobs in the meat industry. This kind of discrimination was never mentioned during the author's field interviews. But the white collar sector is another story. Informants frequently mentioned the complete or nearly complete exclusion of black women from clerical jobs. The available data, although they cannot prove or disprove discrimination, support the allegation of exclusion. In 1968, only 67 of 5,700 female clerical workers in the industry's eight largest firms were Negro.[157]

All firms contacted indicated that they were trying to increase the number of Negro female clerical workers in their employment and, as indicated earlier, some results have been achieved in the last two or three years. Most gains, however, have occurred in the Chicago headquarters offices of the major firms, while the status quo continues at production sites.

It is not possible to determine without much further investigation the motivations for the past discrimination against Negro women (company officials have consistently denied that it ever existed). It may have been based on the belief, referred to earlier, that Negro women tended to have high quit and absentee rates. Or, based on experience, meat packing employers may have decided that Negro women could not work well with other employees. Some of this discriminatory practice may have been

---

[153] *Ibid.*, p. 48.

[154] *Ibid.*, p. 127.

[155] Data in the author's possession.

[156] *Ibid.*

[157] *Ibid.*

part of a general reduction in the female proportion of employment in the industry as a result of union success in sharply raising wage rates on jobs which had traditionally been filled by women. If so, however, black women were much more strongly affected than were white women.

Segregated Facilities

Segregation of blacks from whites in plant service facilities was apparently quite common in the meat industry through World War II. One-third of the locals in the 1949 UPWA survey indicated that the employers with whom they bargained maintained some type of segregated arrangements.[158] Segregated facilities included toilets, washrooms, dressing rooms, eating places, and water fountains.

Purcell found that the Swift plant in Kansas City had segregated dressing rooms for Negro and white women in the early 1950's. The plant cafeteria had been desegregated a few years prior to his study. The Swift plant in East St. Louis had a segregated cafeteria through the late 1950's although it was not segregated by company rule. Swift supported two autonomous employee social organizations in East St. Louis, one for Negroes and one for whites.[159]

The UPWA and some Amalgamated locals during the 1950's pushed hard for desegregation of all plant facilities and in most instances received active cooperation from plant management. Few, if any, plants in the meat industry maintain separate facilities now, since such practices violate the Civil Rights Act of 1964.

Although direct evidence of an empirical nature is not available, the tone of both the UPWA survey and Purcell's study suggests that segregation of white and black workers into separate work groups within departments has not been present in the major meat firms since the 1950's. Because of the uneven distribution of minority persons among departments, however, some de facto segregation continues to exist.

---

[158] Hope, *op. cit.*, p. 30.

[159] Purcell, *Blue Collar Man, op. cit.*, pp. 127-128.

CHAPTER VII

The Future of the Negro in the Meat Industry

In this concluding chapter, the policies and practices are considered which in the foreseeable future will be most important to Negro employment and advancement in the meat industry.

PLANT LOCATION

As has already been noted, many meat packing plants in large cities, located near major terminal markets, have been abandoned since the early 1950's. The four largest meat packing centers during the first half of the century have now been more or less deserted. The first to be closed were the huge facilities in Chicago, followed by most operations in Kansas City and East St. Louis. The death knell very recently sounded again in the packing industry, this time in Omaha. Cudahy closed its meat facilities there in 1967, Armour followed in the spring of 1968 (except for a beef abbatoir), and Swift closed its large plant in that city in November 1969. In addition, many smaller metropolitan facilities have been abandoned since the end of World War II. For example, Swift is closing out most of its St. Paul operations.

The packing plants which replaced these large facilities were built in the 1950's and 1960's and are almost all located in the nonmetropolitan Midwest—in small cities and towns such as West Point, Nebraska; Emporia, Kansas; Worthington, Minnesota; and Cherokee, Iowa. Since few Negroes live in the midwestern hinterlands, the shift in location of meat packing has lowered Negro employment in the industry. But this effect may have been lessened somewhat by the transfer of employees to the new plants from facilities which were closed. The work force of a new plant owned by a major packer is not hired completely from the local community in which it is built. On the contrary, only a small fraction of the workers is usually hired from the local labor market. Job security in the major meat firms has developed to the point where workers are given various forms of protection against plant shutdowns, for example, the right to transfer to new plants if jobs are available there.

Job Protection and Transfer—The Armour Automation Committee

In most of these firms, workers displaced by the closing of facilities who were employed before September 1961 now have preferred claims to jobs in other plants which are held by employees hired after that date. This right, stated in collective bargaining agreements, is in addition to that of first claim to jobs in new plants. Most firms supplement these transfer opportunities by paying moving allowances to employees who do transfer to other plants.

The Armour Automation Committee is the outstanding example of attempts to aid displaced workers by transfer to new plants, as well as by other means. This tripartite arrangement, which includes public experts, was formed in 1959 by Armour, the UPWA, and the Amalgamated in order to deal with the problem of worker displacement brought about by the company's modernization program. Under the program, 20 Armour plants were closed between 1950 and 1965, displacing 13,000 workers.[160] In 1961, the Automation Committee developed the transfer arrangements mentioned above and established procedures to facilitate the transfer of those workers who chose to do so. One such arrangement is "Technological Adjustment Pay" of $65 per week (including unemployment compensation benefits) to workers who are displaced and are awaiting transfer to a new location. Despite the transfer arrangements, few displaced Armour workers have chosen to move to the new plants that have been opened. Only four out of 1,200 displaced workers in Birmingham and Fort Worth decided to transfer, perhaps because the only jobs available at the time were in the North. Greater success was achieved in Sioux City, where 234 out of 1,150 workers transferred to other Armour plants,[161] and, according to informants, transfers from the closed Armour facilities at Kansas City and Omaha have occurred at the same rate. Negotiation of contractual "flow back" rights probably has raised the number of

---

[160] Shultz and Weber, *op. cit.*, p. vii. This book is the best available source for a description of worker displacement experiences under the Automation Committee program.

[161] *Ibid.*, p. 57.

transfers from these cities. These rights permit an employee to take a six-month trial period at the plant to which he transfers. If the employee quits before the six months are up, he will still receive the separation pay to which his company seniority entitles him, less any transfer allowance already paid to him.

Information on the racial composition of workers transferring under the Armour program is just now becoming available; however, it was the impression of most company and union officials that the percentage of displaced black workers who transferred to other meat packing plants is less than the comparable percentage of whites. Several of these officials suggested that Negroes have relatively little enthusiasm for moving to small midwestern cities, especially when these cities are all-white communities, or nearly so.

Nevertheless, some Negroes have transferred to such communities and have had satisfactory experiences working and living in them. Worthington, Minnesota, is the outstanding example of successful transfer of black meat packing workers. Following the opening of a new Armour plant there in the fall of 1964, 41 Negro workers, most of them with families, moved to that rural town of 10,000 from Kansas City and other places where Armour facilities had recently been closed. Worthington had not previously had any black residents, but a careful community program developed by Automation Committee representatives and local civic leaders produced a smooth transition into the community for the Negro workers and their families. Two years later, 35 of the 41 Negro employees still worked in the Worthington plant.[162]

There is no doubt that transfers have been a means of adjustment for only a small number of the meat packing workers who have been displaced since 1950, and it is probable that Negro workers have relied on transfers less frequently than other employees. Thus, the removal of meat packing centers from metropolitan areas to small cities has had the effect of reducing the number and proportion of black workers in the industry. This effect will continue to operate as the industry increases its concentration in lightly populated areas.

It is appropriate to view the closing of meat packing plants in large cities as adding to the complex problems which these

---

[162] James L. Stern, "Adjustment to Plant Closure," *Monthly Labor Review,* Vol. XL (January 1967), pp. 42-46.

cities now face. The additional burden may be very small compared to the totality of urban problems; nevertheless, it is important to note that these plant shutdowns do add to, rather than lessen, the current problems of our cities. This is an ironic fact. Those meat packing firms which relied heavily on Negro migration to Chicago, East St. Louis, Kansas City, and Omaha in order to meet their labor needs during the peak operating periods of World Wars I and II have now moved their plants elsewhere. But the racial and other problems which arose, in large measure, from the manpower needs of these firms (and of the country) remain rooted in the cities. Chicago, East St. Louis, Omaha, and Kansas City all have their ghettoes, and all have experienced major racial disturbances in the 1960's. East St. Louis exemplifies the metamorphosis which has occurred. The industrial base of this city of 80,000 residents has all but disappeared, unemployment among the city's 60,000 blacks is at a very high level, and the city is almost bankrupt.[163]

In the social context of our times, the kind of institutional arrangement provided by the Armour Automation Committee would seem to be the proper responsibility of all major meat packing firms to the cities and to the workers directly affected by plant shutdowns. The Committee's program goes far beyond union-management contractual arrangements in attempting to reduce the adjustment problems of displaced workers. It works through public and private agencies to provide as much job information, counseling, and retraining as possible, having obtained in several instances federal funds for retraining courses. Its laudable efforts to encourage transfers of minority workers to new plants and its attempts to provide smooth adjustment between these workers and their new communities has already been mentioned. These efforts are particularly valuable to minority workers because their problems of adjustment to displacement are more difficult than those of other workers. Research performed for the Committee on the shutdown of meat packing plants in Fort Worth and Oklahoma City has shown that displaced Negroes and Mexicans have greater difficulty in obtaining formal training than do other workers, are more difficult to place in occupations for which they have been trained, and are paid lower wages when they do obtain employment.[164]

---

[163] *Los Angeles Times*, October 20, 1968.

[164] Shultz and Weber, *op. cit.*, pp. 112, 132, 139-141, 167-168.

All of the major meat packers, in their contractual agreements with unions, do have transfer and severance pay provisions which help workers adjust to plant closings. Only Armour, however, has entered into an arrangement—the Automation Committee—which goes well beyond the formal contractual obligations to displaced workers. Although Armour has probably displaced more workers than any other firm because of its modernization program, most large firms, especially Swift, have closed major facilities and will continue to do so. The establishment of programs comparable to those of the Automation Committee by other firms would signify their acceptance of increased responsibility for assisting their own displaced workers and the cities affected by plant shutdowns. And if such programs were provided for most of the industry, more Negro workers would transfer to jobs in new meat plants while those workers who inevitably choose or are forced to remain behind— both black and white—would better exploit the available labor market opportunities.

RECRUITMENT AND SELECTION

At least since 1964, when the major meat packers joined the federal government's Plans for Progress program for the increased utilization of minority workers, the large firms in the meat industry have taken what is now termed affirmative action to recruit job applicants from minority groups, especially Negroes. Practically all of these efforts have been directed to white collar jobs, because the employment of Negroes in this sector has been so limited.

Representatives of the large firms in the industry now visit high schools which have large numbers of black students to solicit applicants for future employment. They also seek Negro applicants through appropriate private and public employment agencies and through Negro community agencies such as the Urban League. Active attempts are made to attract black students in college and university graduating classes as well.

According to our data, these efforts have not achieved a great deal of success; the white collar employment of Negroes in the industry continues to be low by any standard of evaluation. Company spokesmen claim that their efforts to recruit Negroes for white collar positions are hurt by limited supplies of qualified persons and by the comparatively low salaries and status which the industry offers, particularly to college graduates. The predominant view in the industry is that present returns on investment do not warrant the high salaries which would be necessary to attract Negro technicians and professionals now that they are in such great demand; there is little that can be done about the unglamorous nature of the industry, according to the persons with whom the author discussed the situation.

There is no doubt that the Plans for Progress and federal contract compliance programs (all major firms have contracts to supply meat products to the Department of Defense) have been instrumental in bringing about the active recruitment of minority workers which now exists in the industry. Meat packing is an old industry, one not given to innovation in personnel and labor relations policies.[165] Without the pressure of public policy in the area of minority recruitment, it is difficult to believe that the industry would have acted as quickly or extensively as it has.

Employee selection as well as recruitment has been affected by public policies against discrimination and, of course, by the temper of the times. Meat packing firms do not use any formal education requirements for production jobs (although formal education may be given considerable weight in the selection process), with the exception of a few firms which require high school graduation for selection to craft positions. Neither are tests of any kind used, again with the exception of some craft position tests.

Tests

Tests for low-level white collar positions have been eliminated or reduced in number in the large meat industry firms. One firm uses only a typing test for its clerical applicants. Much of this reduction has come about in recent years, undoubtedly as a result of public policies and the general criticism which has arisen against the use of these tests for minority applicants.

Even in selecting applicants for craft positions, the use of tests is much less widespread than before. The president of a local union told the author that some years ago aptitude tests kept black workers from entrance into the craft occupations in his firm. He then asked the company if he could examine all

---

[165] The Armour Automation Commission is an exception. See Harold E. Brooks, "The Armour Automation Commission," *Proceedings of the Twenty-First Annual Winter Meeting, Industrial Relations Research Association, Chicago, December 1968*, pp. 137-143.

test results. At that point the company eliminated the tests and some Negroes are now working in craft positions.

There is widespread feeling among minority persons and some union officials that in the past tests were used to discriminate by keeping Negroes out under the guise of failure to meet selection standards. Where tests are still used for selecting skilled workers, minority employees continue to believe that these tests are discriminatory—that they are not valid indicators of potential job performance. It is also believed that white workers often wish to retain selection tests in order to continue the exclusion of Negroes from craft jobs, and that some local union officials will do nothing to have the tests eliminated because they are in sympathy with their discriminatory effects.

In the future, wherever the representation of Negroes in an occupation is low, tests used to select entrants to that occupation will come under criticism. Firms will be asked to justify their tests, and since few firms have validated them on their own employees, many are likely to eliminate the tests rather than try to justify them. This appears to be happening in the meat industry and the result could be some increase in the number of Negroes employed in craft jobs.

TRAINING

Traditionally, most training in the meat industry has been done on the job. Many production jobs in the industry are of the semiskilled variety, which can be learned in relatively short periods while working with coaching from foremen and fellow workers. The learning period required for performing skilled maintenance work is somewhat longer, but here, too, most of the learning occurs on the job.

With one major exception, significant innovations in the training of minority employees for the meat industry were not found, possibly because of the generally adequate supplies of labor available to most plants. (It should be noted, however, that some meat establishments have a long history of hiring and providing on-the-job training for persons who would now be eligible for manpower programs for the "hard core" unemployed.) Employment in meat packing has been declining; because of plant shutdowns many workers with considerable length of service have been laid off.

Another factor which limits the need for training is the movement of plants out of urban areas, while many of the current government training programs are directed at the hard core disadvantaged in these areas. Meat packing plants have been moving away from these locations for some time now, although many small processing facilities remain in large cities.

Oscar Mayer Program

An exception to the general lack of innovative training in the industry is the program of Oscar Mayer in Chicago. This firm has operated a major meat processing plant in the Near North Side of Chicago since 1883. In recent years the area surrounding the plant has become an all-Negro neighborhood; few whites have remained and many firms have also moved to outlying areas of Chicago. The Oscar Mayer management has decided to stay, however, and has made tentative plans to build a $2 million addition as well. Whether this will be done depends, in part, on the experience of the company in hiring and training local residents. The firm has recently developed a training program for a minimum of 50 hard core unemployed persons, mostly Negroes from the area, in cooperation with the Manpower Administration of the U.S. Department of Labor under the authority and funding of the Manpower Development and Training Act. The fifteen-month program will provide basic orientation to matters such as grooming, money management, and use of transportation facilities; on-the-job training; four hours of basic education a week for as long as 52 weeks; and a large amount of supportive coaching and counseling. Initially the trainees will be employed in relatively low-skilled entry positions at wage rates of over $3.00 an hour. It is one of the purposes of the program, however, to prepare the trainees for upgrading to higher skilled positions, some of which pay well over $4.00 an hour.

Oscar Mayer has also established a similar program for a maximum of 25 persons at its processing plant in a heavily industrialized area of Los Angeles. If these programs are successful, other firms may be encouraged to continue operating their inner city plants and to embark on similar training programs themselves.

REACTION TO EXTERNAL PRESSURE

The rate of job progress of minority persons over the next decade will be determined to a large extent by the ways in which firms react to pressures from organized minority groups and public policies on fair employment. These pressures can now be accurately described as a movement for minority gains. The pace of progress in the absence of the movement would be very slow: firms would have no incentive to do anything out of the ordinary for black and brown workers; therefore, the educational and training disadvantages of these workers would severely limit their progress relative to the rest of the population.

The business community within the last few years has shown signs of an increasingly constructive response to minority group militancy and to the nation's racial crisis. The National Alliance of Businessmen and the Urban Coalition are the most prominent exponents of this response.

The major meat packers, however, are lagging behind most other large firms in their reaction to the pressures for minority job advancement. It is enlightening, in this respect, to quote a recent statement of a management analyst that in meat packing there is "a curious gap between the acknowledgment that conditions are now different, and tough minded management action" to meet the changed conditions.[166] This judgment was well corroborated by the author's own investigations.

The major meat firms are, however, attempting to meet at least their formal obligations under the Civil Rights Act of 1964, the nondiscrimination provisions contained in their contracts with the federal government, and their participation in the Plans for Progress program. Numerous directives for the implementations of equal employment policies were found which had been issued from the general office of a major meat firm to its plant managers. These directives stated in clear and complete terms the affirmative obligations of the plant management to provide equal employment opportunities and the full support of top management for the affirmative actions which must be taken under the law. Still, action must now occur at the plant level, and the record, at least in the area of white collar employment, indicates that plant managers have not been prodded into action by the directives of their headquarters. Indeed, the

---

[166] Meyers, *loc. cit.*, p. 90. See also *Business Week*, Vol. 2087 (August 30, 1969), pp. 82-84.

low level of minority employment which exists in the general offices of the major meat firms may effectively counteract the directives issued to plant managers. If so, the slowly increasing employment of minority persons which is apparently occurring in the general offices may have much more impact on plant management than the formal statements of policy.

The chief executive officer of another major firm has recently made increased hiring of minority persons and improvement in the level of jobs held by minority workers part of the responsibility of all management personnel in the firm. Thus, salary increases and promotions of management persons will be partially influenced by the extent to which they achieve these objectives. Building equal employment goals into the reward structure of the firms will, hopefully, be an effective way of improving minority job status.

As indicated, however, relatively few extraordinary efforts in the areas of recruiting, selection, and training are being made by the big packers. Moreover, many (although certainly not all) industry personnel officials are hostile to the actions of minority organizations and the federal government which are aimed at improving the job experience of minority persons. They generally feel that private groups and the government are unwarrantedly interfering with the right of employers to run their businesses. These industry officials believe that their firms are doing as much for minority persons as the nature of the meat business allows; therefore, the intrusion of outsiders can only serve malicious embarrassment. They believe that inquiries or investigations by outsiders are bound to find inadequacies in minority group programs, because outsiders are not able and do not wish to understand all of the considerations which must be faced to successfully operate firms in the meat industry.

Such attitudes are probably associated with what the industry considers to be a long history of external harassment by private persons and the government. It includes muckracking by Upton Sinclair (*The Jungle*) and other popular writers, numerous investigations of working conditions in stockyards and packing plants, legislation on safety and other conditions of work, numerous antitrust proceedings, meat inspection laws, and requirements to recognize and bargain with unions. Public policy demands for minority employment are seen as another step in a long series of external interference in the meat industry.

The hostility of the major meat firms, while understandable, is hardly a constructive approach at this moment in history. The nation, having finally realized the seriousness of black demands, is now firmly committed, through its public policies, to improving the job experience of minority persons. Government and minority organizations will continue and even step up their demands that major employers do something for minority workers, and where evidence of such effort is not forthcoming, they will apply economic pressure on the unresponsive firms. The managements of meat firms would do well to recognize this trend and to respond willingly to outside concern about the effectiveness of their equal employment policies even when the inner enthusiasm for a willing response may be lacking.

Perhaps more knowledge of the history of Negro employment in their firms would help meat industry officials to better understand both the antagonism and aspirations of black workers. Someone must have observed that the industry lacks a sense of history. This was certainly supported by interviews with meat industry officials; none of them had more than impressionistic knowledge of Negro job experience in their firms prior to the last few years.

SUMMARY AND CONCLUDING REMARKS

The meat industry was one of the first large-scale manufacturing industries to provide jobs for Negroes. The jobs became available to Negroes because undesirable working conditions prevented saturation by whites and because the employment of black workers enabled employers to severely hamper the effective unionization of the meat industry. Under these conditions, the semiskilled nature of most jobs in the industry and migration from the South made possible the employment of many Negroes in the major meat packing centers of the country after 1915. Although black workers obtained jobs in the industry relatively early, they did not obtain job advancement until after World War II, and even then their advancement was limited to skilled manual positions. Until after World War II, the major meat firms were apparently not concerned with Negro job advancement, just as they had not been concerned with the social problems created during World War I by the mass migration of blacks into the communities in which their plants were located.

Now, wages are good in the meat industry ($3.34 an hour for beginning workers under most union contracts in February 1969), working conditions are much improved, and employers are concerned about equal employment goals. In the manual sector of meat industry employment, most equal employment goals have been met. Black workers now have access to all production departments, and in the near future will probably be quite evenly distributed among these departments. They have made substantial advances into skilled craft positions in the last 20 years, and here too, may be expected to attain equitable representation over the next several years. Discrimination against employing Negro women, formerly a common practice in the industry, is now quite rare.

A considerable amount of credit for the nondiscriminatory practices which now prevail in the industry's manual sector should go to the major unions in the industry—the United Packinghouse Workers of America and the Amalgamated Meat Cutters and Butcher Workmen (the two unions merged in 1968). The UPWA placed strong emphasis on ending discrimination against Negroes as soon as it was organized; the Amalgamated followed this example somewhat belatedly, but quite effectively in certain locations, nevertheless. The major firms in the industry generally cooperated with the union efforts for nondiscrimination and, at times, actively aided these efforts. In retrospect, it seems probable that the headquarters managements of these firms were ready by World War II to support equal opportunity goals, but that they were not willing to initiate efforts in this direction. In particular, the major firms were not willing to pressure their local plant managements into ending discriminatory practices. The meat industry firms were much like the Amalgamated union in this respect—they were unable or unwilling to exert influence on local practices. When the UPWA, free from these constraints and inhibitions, provided the impetus for nondiscrimination, the firms were quite willing to cooperate. Finally, credit for the present situation must go to the many black workers who demonstrated, often in the face of considerable hostility, satisfactory job performance.

The nonmanual sector of employment and perhaps foreman positions are the areas in the industry where equal employment goals have not been achieved; black workers comprise about one percent of the industry's white collar employees. Until recently, there has been no external pressure applied for increased hiring of Negroes in nonmanual jobs—few of the industry's white collar workers are represented by a union. Without the outside impetus, meat industry firms, at best, were unconcerned with action to increase Negro employment in office jobs. Many persons who are familiar with the industry believe that discrimination was also commonly practiced against Negro applicants for white collar jobs. Beginning in the early 1960's, the federal government and minority group organizations have, with increasing aggressiveness, urged meat industry firms to employ more black office workers. Judging by the figures, meat firms were somewhat slow to react to these external influences. By 1968, however, the major firms were all engaging in affirmative action, with varying degrees of enthusiasm, to raise minority white collar employment. The industry has increased its employment of Negro office workers in the last few years, but it started from a very low base and, of course, is now competing with other industries for the limited supply of blacks who are qualified for this kind of employment. Without considerably more aggressive recruiting and training than has been undertaken thus far, it is doubtful that the meat industry will be able to raise its Negro proportion of nonmanual employment to even three percent in the forseeable future. Substantial increments in the supply of Negro white collar workers would, of course, affect the accuracy of that prediction.

It must be emphasized that external pressure has clearly been an important influence on minority employment policies in the meat industry. This is shown, first, by the success of the UPWA and the Amalgamated in largely eliminating, between World War II and 1960, discriminatory practices of long standing in many meat plants—practices which the executive managements of the meat firms probably also wished to eliminate, but did not until the unions' nondiscrimination policies were asserted. It is shown, also, by the recent efforts of meat firms to hire more Negro white collar workers in response to public policies and minority group militancy. Three agencies of the federal government—the Defense Supply Agency (contract compliance reviews), the voluntary Plans for Progress organization, and the Equal Employment Opportunity Commission—now monitor the equal employment practices of the major meat firms (and most other major firms as well), and, according to the firms themselves, have had an impact on employment practices. Industry officials deny that minority group organizations have had any direct impact on their practices. The indirect effects have probably been significant, however, because these organizations have helped to create a climate of community and national opinion such that failure of a firm to take affirmative action on minority employment incurs the risk of severe criticism from at least some representatives of the public, self-proclaimed or otherwise.

In view of the improvements in minority employment policies and practices which have occurred and are continuing to occur, it is somewhat ironic that the meat industry is undergoing structural changes which threaten, or, at least diminish the attractiveness of, Negro job opportunities. Jobs in the meat packing division, which contains the industry's largest firms and which has the most advanced minority employment practices, are disappearing as a result of technological progress. Most of those which remain are located in cities which have few black residents.

Having recently migrated to the big cities in search of economic opportunities, few Negroes are likely to move to the small midwestern cities to which meat packing plants are being shifted, even though the prospects for economic and social progress may be better there. The migration of whites from large to small cities is very limited; there is even less likelihood that blacks will undertake this kind of move since so few Negroes live in most small midwestern cities at present. The number of jobs held by Negroes in poultry plants and in other small meat establishments in the South will increase in the years ahead, but these jobs are much less desirable than those which are being lost in northern meat packing plants.

Appendix

STATISTICAL DATA

TABLE A-1. Meat Industry
Total and Negro Employment by Sex
1910-1960

	Male			Female		
	Total	Negro	Percent Negro	Total	Negro	Percent Negro
1910	88,600	5,600	6.3	5,800	200	3.4
1920[a] (Operatives and laborers)	120,200	26,100	21.7	12,200	2,200	18.0
(Estimate for all occupations)	178,800	27,800	15.5	19,100	2,200	11.5
1930	152,700	19,000	12.4	20,900	1,400	6.7
1940[b]	178,400	15,000	8.4	31,700	1,200	2.5
1950[b]	217,900	32,800	15.1	50,000	6,300	11.3
1960[b]	240,900	34,000	14.1	77,200	9,900	12.8

Source: U.S. Census of Population:

1910, Vol. IV, Occupations.
1920, Vol. IV, Occupations.
1930, Vol. IV, Occupations, U.S. Summary, Table 13.
1940, Vol. III, The Labor Force, Part 1, Table 76.
1950, Vol. II, Characteristics of the Population, Part 1, Table 33.
1960, PC (1) D, Detailed Characteristics, Part 1, Table 213.

Note: 1910-30 data are for persons, age 10 and over, who usually worked in "slaughtering," packing houses and meat packing, or as stockyard laborers. Many persons who were returned by the censuses of 1910, 1920, and 1930 as "stockyard laborers" (a wholesale trade classification), were actually employed by meat packing firms, especially in Chicago where "the frequent use of the term 'stockyard' for 'meat packing house' . . . made difficult the proper classification of the meat packing house employees of that City." (U.S. Census of Population, 1920, Vol. IV, Occupations, p. 15. For stockyard laborers, see Table A-2.

[a] The 1920 estimate of employment in all occupations was made by applying the average of the 1910 and 1930 ratios of total employment to operative and laborer employment (for all persons and Negroes), to the 1920 employment of operatives and laborers as given by the 1920 census.

[b] For persons, age 14 and over, employed in meat products manufacturing.

TABLE A-2. *Stockyard Laborers,*
U.S. and Chicago, Total and Negro Employment
1910-1930

	All Persons	Negro	Percent Negro
1910 U.S.	6,000	540	9.0
Chicago	3,050	180	5.9
1920 U.S.	22,890	6,030	26.3
Chicago	16,500	5,300	32.1
1930 U.S.	8,740	1,980	22.7
Chicago	4,820	1,650	34.2

Source: *U.S. Census of Population:*

1910, Vol. IV, *Occupations.*
1920, Vol. IV, *Occupations.*
1930, Vol. IV, *Occupations.*

TABLE A-3. *Meat Packing*

Production Worker Employment by Region and for Selected States, 1919-1963

Region	Production Workers ('000)						Percent of U. S. Total					
	1919	1929	1939[a]	1947	1953	1963	1919	1929	1939	1947	1958	1963
Northeast	19.9	18.6	16.8	18.2	14.4	11.8	12.4	15.2	14.0	10.9	9.5	8.5
East North Central[b]	70.1	45.6	39.6	47.1	36.2	27.4	43.5	37.2	33.0	28.2	24.0	19.8
West North Central[c]	50.7	38.4	38.9	59.3	54.9	52.8	31.5	31.4	32.4	35.5	36.4	38.2
South	12.1	11.6	15.4	26.7	31.2	31.7	7.5	9.4	12.8	16.0	20.7	22.9
West	8.1	8.3	9.2	15.8	14.1	14.7	5.1	6.8	7.7	9.5	9.4	10.6
U.S. total	160.9	122.5	119.9	167.1	150.8	138.4	100.0	100.0	99.9	100.1	100.0	100.0
Selected States:												
Illinois	54.2	29.6	23.5	24.2	12.0	7.5	33.7	24.2	19.6	14.5	8.0	5.4
Kansas	17.8	9.1	7.4	10.7	6.1	6.2	11.1	7.4	6.2	6.4	4.0	4.5
Missouri	8.3	5.6	4.5	7.5	6.2	5.8	5.1	4.6	3.7	4.5	4.1	4.2
Nebraska	10.1	6.1	4.7	7.8	8.6	8.2	6.3	5.0	3.9	4.7	5.7	5.9
Iowa	7.1	8.7	11.0	18.5	19.1	18.5	4.4	7.1	9.2	11.1	12.7	13.3
Minnesota	5.2	6.9	8.8	11.2	10.8	10.3	3.2	5.6	7.4	6.7	7.2	7.4

Source: *U. S. Census of Manufactures:*

1929, Vol. II, *Reports by Industries,* Meat Packing, Table 2. (For 1919 and 1929.)
1939, Vol. II, *Reports by Industries,* Part I, Meat Packing, Table 2.
1947, Vol. II, *Statistics by Industry,* Meat Products, Table 2.
1958, Vol. II, *Industry Statistics,* Part 1, Meat Products, Table 2.
1963, Vol. II, *Industry Statistics,* Part 1, Meat Products, Table 2.

[a] 1939 total was later revised by the Bureau of the Census to 115.0; however, regional revisions are not available.

[b] Includes Illinois, Indiana, Michigan, Ohio, and Wisconsin.

[c] Includes Iowa, Kansas, Minnesota, Missouri, Nebraska, North Dakota, and South Dakota.

TABLE A-4. *Meat Industry*
Employment by Standard Industrial Classification
1958-1968 (000)

	Total Industry	Meat Packing	Meat Processing	Poultry Processing
1958	319.4	215.1	44.0	60.3
1959	317.1	207.5	45.5	64.2
1960	322.6	200.9	47.5	65.2
1961	319.5	202.7	47.4	69.5
1962	315.9	198.3	47.7	69.9
1963	316.5	195.4	50.1	71.0
1964	316.2	193.9	51.9	70.3
1965	318.4	193.3	52.0	73.1
1966	323.9	189.1	52.6	82.3
1967	329.1	187.8	54.5	86.8
1968	330.0	187.2	55.7	87.1

Source: U. S. Bureau of Labor Statistics, *Employment and Earnings Statistics for the United States, 1909-68*, Bulletin 1312-6, 1968; and *Employment and Earnings*, Vol. 15 (March 1969), Table B-2. The definition of employment used by this source and the method of obtaining data differ from those used in obtaining employment figures for the *U. S. Census of Manufactures*. The latter was the source for the comparable tables in the text.

TABLE A-5. *Meat Industry*
Employment in Chicago and Greater Kansas City
1899-1963

	Chicago	Kansas City
1899	29,550	9,487
1909	27,147	10,656
1919	52,423	20,339
1929	29,463	9,035
1939	28,229	7,443
1947	31,931	10,086
1958	18,075	5,816
1963	10,940 [a]	5,555

Source: *U. S. Census of Manufactures:*

1899, Vol. VII, *Manufactures,* Part II, *States and Territories,* Illinois, Table 8.

1909, Vol. IX, *Reports by States,* Illinois, Table 1; Kansas, Table 1 (for 1899 and 1909).

1919, Vol. IX, *Reports for States,* Illinois, Table 43; Kansas, Table 30.

1929, Vol. III, *Reports by States,* Illinois and Missouri, Table 13.

1939, Vol. III, *Reports for States,* Illinois and Missouri, Table 9.

1947, Vol. III, *Statistics by States,* Illinois and Missouri, Table 6.

1963, Vol. III, *Area Statistics,* Illinois and Missouri, Table 6 (for 1963 and 1958).

Note: Data for 1899-1919 are for Kansas City, Kansas only; no "slaughtering" employment is given for Kansas City, Missouri.

[a] Of this number, 3,354 were employed in meat packing plants.

TABLE A-6.

Meat Industry, Northeast Region

Employment by Race, Sex, and Occupational Group

205 Establishments, 1964

Occupation	All Employees			Male			Female		
	Total	Negro	Percent Negro	Total	Negro	Percent Negro	Total	Negro	Percent Negro
Officials and managers	315	2	0.6	313	2	0.6	2	0	0.0
Professionals	75	1	1.3	74	1	1.4	1	0	0.0
Technicians	37	2	5.4	28	2	7.1	9	0	0.0
Sales workers	389	2	0.5	385	2	0.5	4	0	0.0
Office and clerical	381	3	0.8	212	3	1.4	169	0	0.0
Total white collar	1,197	10	0.8	1,012	10	1.0	185	0	0.0
Craftsmen	641	65	10.1	641	65	10.1	0	0	0.0
Operatives	2,110	347	16.4	1,657	322	19.4	453	25	5.5
Laborers	776	114	14.7	575	98	17.0	201	16	8.0
Service workers	277	23	8.3	196	22	11.2	81	1	1.2
Total blue collar	3,804	549	14.4	3,069	507	16.5	735	42	5.7
Total	5,001	559	11.2	4,081	517	12.7	920	42	4.6

Source: Data in the author's possession.

Note: For regional definitions, see Table 4, p. 9.

TABLE A-7.
Meat Industry, North Central Region
Employment by Race, Sex, and Occupational Group
205 Establishments, 1964

Occupation	All Employees			Male			Female		
	Total	Negro	Percent Negro	Total	Negro	Percent Negro	Total	Negro	Percent Negro
Officials and managers	5,034	9	0.2	5,005	9	0.2	29	0	0.0
Professionals	1,799	14	0.8	1,732	12	0.7	67	2	3.0
Technicians	761	6	0.8	676	4	0.6	85	2	2.4
Sales workers	3,154	4	0.1	3,085	4	0.1	69	0	0.0
Office and clerical	6,026	52	0.9	2,923	30	1.0	3,103	22	0.7
Total white collar	16,774	85	0.5	13,421	59	0.4	3,353	26	0.8
Craftsmen	9,269	1,225	13.2	8,956	1,189	13.3	313	36	11.5
Operatives	30,745	4,546	14.8	25,218	4,085	16.2	5,527	461	8.3
Laborers	10,409	1,939	18.6	7,993	1,627	20.4	2,416	312	12.9
Service workers	1,637	273	16.7	1,435	268	18.7	202	5	2.5
Total blue collar	50,060	7,983	15.3	43,602	7,169	16.4	8,458	814	9.6
Total	68,834	8,068	11.7	57,023	7,228	12.7	11,811	840	7.1

Source: Data in the author's possession.

Note: For regional definitions, see Table 4, p. 9.

TABLE A-8.

Meat Industry, Southern Region

Employment by Race, Sex, and Occupational Group

205 Establishments, 1964

Occupation	All Employees			Male			Female		
	Total	Negro	Percent Negro	Total	Negro	Percent Negro	Total	Negro	Percent Negro
Officials and managers	1,316	14	1.1	1,306	14	1.1	10	0	0.0
Professionals	251	3	1.2	238	3	1.3	13	0	0.0
Technicians	65	1	1.5	48	1	2.1	17	0	0.0
Sales workers	714	0	0.0	709	0	0.0	5	0	0.0
Office and clerical	1,203	2	0.2	553	0	0.0	650	2	0.3
Total white collar	3,549	20	0.6	2,854	18	0.6	695	2	0.3
Craftsmen	2,307	341	14.8	2,282	336	14.7	25	5	20.0
Operatives	4,784	1,003	21.0	3,978	902	22.7	806	101	12.5
Laborers	11,224	3,091	27.5	5,973	1,701	28.5	5,251	1,390	26.5
Service workers	311	127	40.8	286	111	38.8	25	16	64.0
Total blue collar	18,626	4,562	24.5	12,519	3,050	24.4	6,107	1,512	24.8
Total	22,175	4,582	20.7	15,373	3,068	20.0	6,802	1,514	22.3

Source: Data in the author's possession.

Note: For regional definitions, see Table 4, p. 9.

TABLE A-9.
Meat Industry, Western Region
Employment by Race, Sex, and Occupational Group
205 Establishments, 1964

Occupation	All Employees			Male			Female		
	Total	Negro	Percent Negro	Total	Negro	Percent Negro	Total	Negro	Percent Negro
Officials and managers	631	0	0.0	630	0	0.0	1	0	0.0
Professionals	92	0	0.0	89	0	0.0	3	0	0.0
Technicians	47	2	4.3	33	2	6.1	14	0	0.0
Sales workers	642	1	0.2	622	1	0.2	20	0	0.0
Office and clerical	815	3	0.4	401	0	0.0	414	3	0.7
Total white collar	2,227	6	0.3	1,775	3	0.2	452	3	0.7
Craftsmen	1,673	150	9.0	1,617	149	9.2	56	1	1.8
Operatives	3,161	313	9.9	2,534	299	11.8	627	14	2.2
Laborers	1,793	171	9.5	1,059	157	14.8	734	14	1.9
Service workers	159	31	19.5	156	31	19.9	3	0	0.0
Total blue collar	6,786	665	9.8	5,366	636	11.9	1,420	29	2.0
Total	9,013	671	7.4	1,141	639	8.9	1,872	32	1.7

Source: Data in the author's possession.

Note: For regional definitions, see Table 4, p. 9.

TABLE A-10.
Meat Industry, Northeast Region
Employment by Race, Sex, and Occupational Group
252 Establishments, 1966

Occupation	All Employees			Male			Female		
	Total	Negro	Percent Negro	Total	Negro	Percent Negro	Total	Negro	Percent Negro
Officials and managers	423	2	0.5	421	2	0.5	2	0	0.0
Professionals	75	0	0.0	75	0	0.0	0	0	0.0
Technicians	44	2	4.5	38	2	5.3	6	0	0.0
Sales workers	478	2	0.4	474	2	0.4	4	0	0.0
Office and clerical	517	18	3.5	266	13	4.9	251	5	2.0
Total white collar	1,537	24	1.6	1,274	19	1.5	263	5	1.9
Craftsmen	703	66	9.4	700	65	9.3	3	1	33.3
Operatives	2,302	403	17.5	1,836	349	19.0	466	54	11.6
Laborers	1,702	316	18.6	1,117	214	19.2	585	102	17.4
Service workers	128	26	20.3	123	26	21.1	5	0	0.0
Total blue collar	4,835	811	16.8	3,776	654	17.3	1,059	157	14.8
Total	6,372	835	13.1	5,050	673	13.3	1,322	162	12.3

Source: Data in the author's possession.

Note: For regional definitions, see Table 4, p. 9.

TABLE A-11.

Meat Industry, North Central Region

Employment by Race, Sex, and Occupational Group

252 Establishments, 1966

Occupation	All Employees			Male			Female		
	Total	Negro	Percent Negro	Total	Negro	Percent Negro	Total	Negro	Percent Negro
Officials and managers	5,434	23	0.4	5,397	22	0.4	37	1	2.7
Professionals	1,502	5	0.3	1,439	5	0.3	63	0	0.0
Technicians	901	10	1.1	790	9	1.1	111	1	0.9
Sales workers	3,191	9	0.3	3,126	9	0.3	65	0	0.0
Office and clerical	6,152	59	1.0	2,933	32	1.1	3,219	27	0.8
Total white collar	17,180	106	0.6	13,685	77	0.6	3,495	29	0.8
Craftsmen	9,593	1,012	10.5	9,366	1,008	10.8	227	4	1.8
Operatives	30,462	4,118	13.5	25,762	3,721	14.4	4,700	397	8.4
Laborers	12,096	1,617	13.4	9,192	1,465	15.9	2,904	152	5.2
Service workers	1,938	286	14.8	1,718	276	16.1	220	10	4.5
Total blue collar	54,089	7,033	13.0	46,038	6,470	14.1	8,051	563	7.0
Total	71,269	7,139	10.0	59,723	6,547	11.0	11,546	592	5.1

Source: Data in the author's possession.

Note: For regional definitions, see Table 4, p. 9.

TABLE A-12.
Meat Industry, Southern Region
Employment by Race, Sex, and Occupational Group
252 Establishments, 1966

Occupation	All Employees			Male			Female		
	Total	Negro	Percent Negro	Total	Negro	Percent Negro	Total	Negro	Percent Negro
Officials and managers	1,568	13	0.8	1,556	13	0.8	12	0	0.0
Professionals	159	19	11.9	156	19	12.2	3	0	0.0
Technicians	114	0	0.0	94	0	0.0	20	0	0.0
Sales workers	1,067	0	0.0	1,059	0	0.0	8	0	0.0
Office and clerical	1,591	18	1.1	772	13	1.7	819	5	0.6
Total white collar	4,499	50	1.1	3,637	45	1.2	862	5	0.6
Craftsmen	2,488	478	19.2	2,462	476	19.3	26	2	7.7
Operatives	6,279	1,819	29.0	5,263	1,470	27.9	1,016	349	34.4
Laborers	11,885	3,881	32.7	5,974	2,066	34.6	5,911	1,815	30.7
Service workers	371	185	49.9	329	164	49.8	42	21	50.0
Total blue collar	21,023	6,363	30.3	14,028	4,176	29.8	6,995	2,187	31.3
Total	25,522	6,413	25.1	17,665	4,221	23.9	7,857	2,192	27.9

Source: Data in the author's possession.

Note: For regional definitions, see Table 4, p. 9.

TABLE A-13.
Meat Industry, Western Region
Employment by Race, Sex, and Occupational Group
252 Establishments, 1966

Occupation	All Employees			Male			Female		
	Total	Negro	Percent Negro	Total	Negro	Percent Negro	Total	Negro	Percent Negro
Officials and managers	541	1	0.2	538	1	0.2	3	0	0.0
Professionals	88	0	0.0	85	0	0.0	3	0	0.0
Technicians	31	0	0.0	19	0	0.0	12	0	0.0
Sales workers	572	2	0.3	543	2	0.4	29	0	0.0
Office and clerical	600	2	0.3	262	1	0.4	338	1	0.3
Total white collar	1,832	5	0.3	1,447	4	0.3	385	1	0.3
Craftsmen	1,764	136	7.7	1,709	135	7.9	55	1	1.8
Operatives	2,397	190	7.9	1,887	170	9.0	510	20	3.9
Laborers	1,496	158	10.6	1,036	150	14.5	460	8	1.7
Service workers	182	49	26.9	174	49	28.2	8	0	0.0
Total blue collar	5,839	533	9.1	4,806	504	10.5	1,033	29	2.8
Total	7,671	538	7.0	6,253	508	8.1	1,418	30	2.1

Source: Data in the author's possession.

Note: For regional definitions, see Table 4, p. 9.

TABLE A-14.
Meat Industry, Northeast Region
Employment by Race, Sex, and Occupational Group
252 Establishments, 1968

Occupation	All Employees			Male			Female		
	Total	Negro	Percent Negro	Total	Negro	Percent Negro	Total	Negro	Percent Negro
Officials and managers	495	13	2.6	491	13	2.6	4	0	0.0
Professionals	85	0	0.0	82	0	0.0	3	0	0.0
Technicians	48	4	8.3	44	4	9.1	4	0	0.0
Sales workers	436	7	1.6	429	7	1.6	7	0	0.0
Office and clerical	537	20	3.7	232	10	4.3	305	10	3.3
Total white collar	1,601	44	2.7	1,278	34	2.7	323	10	3.1
Craftsmen	733	74	10.1	684	74	10.8	49	0	0.0
Operatives	2,317	428	18.5	1,897	364	19.2	420	64	15.2
Laborers	1,547	364	23.5	971	262	27.0	576	102	17.7
Service workers	113	17	15.0	109	17	15.6	4	0	0.0
Total blue collar	4,710	883	18.7	3,661	717	19.6	1,049	166	15.8
Total	6,311	927	14.7	4,939	751	15.2	1,372	176	12.8

Source: Data in the author's possession.

Note: For regional definitions, see Table 4, p. 9.

TABLE A-15.
Meat Industry, North Central Region
Employment by Race, Sex, and Occupational Group
252 Establishments, 1968

Occupation	All Employees			Male			Female		
	Total	Negro	Percent Negro	Total	Negro	Percent Negro	Total	Negro	Percent Negro
Officials and managers	5,591	33	0.6	5,555	32	0.6	36	1	2.8
Professionals	1,486	9	0.6	1,399	9	0.6	87	0	0.0
Technicians	878	17	1.9	785	14	1.8	93	3	3.2
Sales workers	2,776	14	0.5	2,715	13	0.5	61	1	1.6
Office and clerical	5,854	111	1.9	2,590	58	2.2	3,264	53	1.6
Total white collar	16,585	184	1.1	13,044	126	1.0	3,541	58	1.6
Craftsmen	9,229	936	10.1	9,119	922	10.1	110	14	12.7
Operatives	32,127	4,411	13.7	26,758	3,939	14.7	5,369	472	8.8
Laborers	11,769	1,331	11.3	8,932	1,168	13.1	2,837	163	5.7
Service workers	1,574	224	14.2	1,400	216	15.4	174	8	4.6
Total blue collar	54,699	6,902	12.6	46,209	6,245	13.5	8,490	657	7.7
Total	71,284	7,086	9.9	59,253	6,371	10.8	12,031	715	5.9

Source: Data in the author's possession.

Note: For regional definitions, see Table 4, p. 9.

TABLE A-16.

Meat Industry, Southern Region

Employment by Race, Sex, and Occupational Group

252 Establishments, 1968

Occupation	All Employees			Male			Female		
	Total	Negro	Percent Negro	Total	Negro	Percent Negro	Total	Negro	Percent Negro
Officials and managers	1,729	51	2.8	1,775	50	2.8	22	1	4.5
Professionals	242	2	0.8	227	1	0.4	15	1	6.7
Technicians	103	1	1.0	86	1	1.2	17	0	0.0
Sales workers	1,044	0	0.0	1,027	0	0.0	17	0	0.0
Office and clerical	1,569	102	6.5	681	21	3.1	888	81	9.1
Total white collar	4,755	156	3.3	3,796	73	1.9	959	83	8.7
Craftsmen	2,623	554	21.1	2,591	542	20.9	32	12	37.5
Operatives	8,379	2,729	32.6	6,478	2,044	31.6	1,901	685	36.0
Laborers	11,788	4,145	35.2	5,837	2,136	36.6	5,951	2,009	33.8
Service workers	330	185	56.1	304	168	55.3	26	17	65.4
Total blue collar	23,120	7,613	32.9	15,210	4,890	32.1	7,910	2,723	34.4
Total	27,875	7,769	27.9	19,006	4,963	26.1	8,869	2,806	31.6

Source: Data in the author's possession.

Note: For regional definitions, see Table 4, p. 9.

TABLE A-17.

Meat Industry, Western Region

Employment by Race, Sex, and Occupational Group

252 Establishments, 1968

Occupation	All Employees			Male			Female		
	Total	Negro	Percent Negro	Total	Negro	Percent Negro	Total	Negro	Percent Negro
Officials and managers	562	1	0.2	557	1	0.2	5	0	0.0
Professionals	89	0	0.0	84	0	0.0	5	0	0.0
Technicians	81	13	16.0	71	13	18.3	10	0	0.0
Sales workers	553	3	0.5	539	3	0.6	14	0	0.0
Office and clerical	616	6	1.0	244	2	0.8	372	4	1.1
Total white collar	1,901	23	1.2	1,495	19	1.3	406	4	1.0
Craftsmen	1,709	151	8.8	1,669	144	8.6	40	7	17.5
Operatives	2,423	221	9.1	1,873	188	10.0	550	33	6.0
Laborers	1,648	153	9.3	1,177	141	12.0	471	12	2.5
Service workers	148	26	17.6	140	26	18.6	8	0	0.0
Total blue collar	5,928	551	9.3	4,859	499	10.3	1,069	52	4.9
Total	7,829	574	7.3	6,354	518	8.2	1,475	56	3.8

Source: Data in the author's possession.

Note: For regional definitions, see Table 4, p. 9.

Index

Abbott, Edith, 87n
Absenteeism, 98-99
Age, Arthur V., 42n
Alschuler, Judge Samuel S., 34
Aluminum Ore Co., 39
Amalgamated Meat Cutters and Butcher Workmen of North America, 15-16, 30-33, 67, 71-73, 112
  Local 651, 31
  racial policies of, 33, 68-69, 71-72, 103, 110, 122-123
  and strikes, 19-21, 34
American Beef Packers, 7
American Federation of Labor (AFL), 15, 31
American Meat Institute, 4n
American Unity Labor Union, 32
Armour and Co., 41, 45, 56, 58, 62-63, 89, 94, 103n, 111
  strikes against, 32, 39, 69
Armour Automation Committee, 112-115
Arnould, Richard J., 58n, 62n, 63n
Ashland Avenue Business Men's Association, 22

Ballweg, John A., 106n
Bittner, Van, 67
Breckinridge, Sophonisba P., 37n
Brody, David, 18n, 31n, 34n, 41n, 67n, 68n, 69n
Brooks, Harold E., 116n
Business Week 78n, 19n

Chicago Commission on Race Relations, 27n, 30n, 32n, 36n, 37n, 41n, 84, 84n
Chicago Defender, 26
Chicago Federation of Labor, 23n, 31
Civil Rights Act of 1964, 110, 119
Clayton, Horace R., 69n
Commons, John R., 18n, 21n, 97n
Comstock, Alzada P., 38n
Congress of Industrial Organizations (CIO), 16, 67-69
Consumption of meat products, 10
  poultry, 57
Cudahy Company, 41, 58, 62, 111

De Graff, Herrell, 56n
Derber, Milton, 56n
Douty, H. M., 61n
Dubin, R., 37n

East St. Louis Central Trades and Labor Union, 39-40
Eckhaus, R. S., 13n
Employment, 10-16, 44-45, 49
  1870-1914, 17-25
  1930's, 49-52
  1940's, 52
  1947-1960, 55-57, 59-62
  female, 13-14, 53
  in South, 51-52, 59, 61
  in West North Central, 59
Equal Employment Opportunity Commission, 94n, 95n, 123
Equal employment policies, 119-122

Fabricant, Solomon, 44n, 45n
Fitzpatrick, John, 23n
Foster, William Z., 30, 30n

Gompers, Samuel, 31

Harding, Myrick D., 45n
Harris, Abram, 21n, 22n, 29n, 31n, 32n, 35n, 36n
Harris, Don, 67
Herbst, Alma, 17n, 18n, 19n, 20n, 21n, 22n, 23n, 29n, 30n, 31n, 32n, 34n, 35n, 36n, 41n, 50n, 86n, 97n, 98n, 105n
Hope, John II, 68n, 96n, 99n, 100n, 102n, 105n, 110n
Hormel, George A. and Co., 57, 62
Hygrade Food Products Corp., 62

Industrial structure, 4-9
  impact of conglomerates, 7
Industry earnings, 4-7, 63
Industry decentralization, 7-8, 47-48, 57-62
  displacement, 112-115
  effect on Negro population, 7, 14, 66, 74

143

INDUSTRIAL RESEARCH UNIT
WHARTON SCHOOL OF FINANCE AND COMMERCE
UNIVERSITY OF PENNSYLVANIA

Founded in 1921 as a separate Wharton Department, the Industrial Research Unit has a long record of publication and research in the labor market, productivity, union relations, and business report fields. Major Industrial Research Unit studies are published as research projects are completed. Advanced research reports are issued as appropriate in a general or special series.

Recent Industrial Research Unit Studies

(Available from the University of Pennsylvania Press or the Industrial Research Unit)

No. 40   Gladys L. Palmer, *et al.*, *The Reluctant Job Changer* (1962) $7.50.

No. 41   George M. Parks, *The Economics of Carpeting and Resilient Flooring: An Evaluation and Comparison* (1966) $5.00.

No. 42   Michael H. Moskow, *Teachers and Unions: The Applicability of Bargaining to Public Education* (1966) $8.50.

No. 43   F. Marion Fletcher, *Market Restraints in the Retail Drug Industry* (1967) $10.00.

No. 44   Herbert R. Northrup and Gordon R. Storholm, *Restrictive Labor Practices in the Supermarket Industry* (1967) $7.50.

No. 45   William N. Chernish, *Coalition Bargaining: A Study of Union Tactics and Public Policy* (1969) $7.95.

No. 46   Herbert R. Northrup, Richard L. Rowan, *et al.*, *Negro Employment in Basic Industry. A Study of Racial Policies in Six Industries.* (Also Vol. I Studies of Negro Employment.) (1970) $10.00.

Nos. 1-39   Available from Kraus Reprint Co., 16 East 46th St., New York, N.Y. 10017.

Research Reports

Racial Policies in American Industry Series

1. *The Negro in the Automobile Industry*, by Herbert R. Northrup.
   1968. $2.50
2. *The Negro in the Aerospace Industry*, by Herbert R. Northrup.
   1968. $2.50
3. *The Negro in the Steel Industry*, by Richard L. Rowan.   1968. $3.50
4. *The Negro in the Hotel Industry*, by Edward C. Koziara
   and Karen S. Koziara.   1968. $2.50
5. *The Negro in the Petroleum Industry*, by Carl B. King and
   Howard W. Risher, Jr.   1969. $3.50
6. *The Negro in the Rubber Tire Industry*, by Herbert R. Northrup
   and Alan B. Batchelder.   1969. $3.50
7. *The Negro in the Chemical Industry*, by William Howard Quay, Jr.
   1969. $3.50
8. *The Negro in the Paper Industry*, by Herbert R. Northrup.   1969. $8.50
9. *The Negro in the Banking Industry*, by Armand J. Thieblot, Jr.
   1970. $5.95
10. *The Negro in the Insurance Industry*, by Linda P. Fletcher. 1970. $5.95
11. *The Negro in the Public Utilities Industries*, by Bernard E. Anderson.
    1970. $5.95
12. *The Negro in the Meat Industry*, by Walter A. Fogel   1970. $4.50
13. *The Negro in the Tobacco Industry*, by Herbert R. Northrup. 1970. $4.50

Forthcoming Racial Policies studies will include textiles, various retail trades, motor truck, rail and air transportation, urban transit and ship-building.

Labor Relations and Public Policy Series

1. *Compulsory Arbitration and the NLRB*, by Paul A. Abodeely, 1968. $2.50
2. *Union Authorization Cards and the NLRB*,
   by Alan R. McFarland and Wayne S. Bishop.   1969. $2.50

Forthcoming studies will deal with various aspects of government labor policy including bargaining unit determination, picketing and boycott regulation, and government intervention in labor disputes.

Miscellaneous Series

14. *Economics of Carpeting and Resilient Flooring: A Survey of Published Material and a Questionnaire Summary*, by David C. Stewart. 1966. $1.00
15. *Job Mobility and Occupational Change: Philadelphia Male Workers, 1940-1960*, by Carol P. Brainerd.   1966. $2.00
16. *Improving the Potential for Negro Employment and Skill Development in the Delaware Valley Fabricated Metals Industry*, by Armand J. Thieblot, Jr., and William N. Chernish.   1967. $2.00

Order from University of Pennsylvania Press, or the Industrial Research Unit, Philadelphia, Pennsylvania 19104